Making

Waves

Making

Waves

Floating Homes and Life on the Water

Portland Mitchell

with 225 illustrations

Renovating & Decorating — 128

Creative Channels — 176

When I first sent out this book proposal, I had no idea what an incredible journey it would take me on. To say I am inspired

by the boat-dwellers within its pages is an understatement – they have helped me rediscover a thrill and excitement that took me back to my childhood in Africa, when, aged six, I would crew for my dad. We raced our Enterprise sailing dinghy across the sun-splashed waves of a shallow *dambo*, accompanied by the sound of lapping water. Since I was there purely to make up the numbers, I soaked up the sunshine and sense of freedom you don't get on land.

Years later, we moved from Zambia to Scotland. The weather wasn't as favourable for sailors, but my parents had succumbed to the boating bug and soon bought a wooden cabin cruiser called *Aquarius*. This fine vessel, moored at Balloch on Loch Lomond, would only motor backwards and rain leaked into the cabins, which my sister and I would collect in strategically placed pots and pans, listening to the musical drip, drip, drip of the raindrops.

We spent every moment we could on *Aquarius*, huddled around the log-burner on chilly days, or basking in the sun on the few hot days Scotland had to offer. We caught minnows

in jam jars, built bonfires and retrieved baked potatoes from the hot ashes. There was no technology, just a radio, plenty of books, a lot of imagination and an immense sense of freedom and adventure. I live in London now, surrounded by technology and pollution, and so much stuff that it spills out of the loft, the garden shed and the garage.

Introduction

I love my little home, my family, the hubbub of city life –
the beauty of its architecture and the way it breathes culture
into my very soul – but also yearn for the calm reassurance
that being by the water brings me. I've found myself drawn
to canals and boatyards, and fantasize about living on a
boat, rediscovering the very essence that takes me back to
a simpler, less high-tech world than the one we have created
for ourselves.

Making Waves celebrates those who have managed to
achieve this harmonious balance, discovered how to live in
the modern world and yet hold present-day paraphernalia at
bay. Their homes are water-borne, magnificent, stylish and
freeing, and they have my envy and admiration, and are my

Oldenburg, Denmark

inspiration in equal measure. Each boat
included here affords its dwellers a beautifully
proportioned retreat; some glide through
extraordinary countryside, while others bob
companionably in city wharfs. Their interiors
reflect their inhabitants' imaginations,
families, working lives, and how every inch
has been considered and fully utilized
to create unique and absorbing places in which to live. These
homes are personal statements that are as fluid as the waters
on which they float.

Stødig cruises serenely along the calm waters near Tromsø, Norway.

Life on the water has always been about making the most of what you've got, from repurposing a rope to restoring and redeploying a weatherbeaten canvas. Now, a new generation of boat-dwellers are taking things to another level, bringing everything from a rescued shipping container to a houseboat built from recycled materials onto the world's waterways.

Green Credentials

A Clean Sweep
Feniks, Netherlands

There are a few things you need to know about Pieter Kool and Stefanie Hakkesteegt. First and foremost, that they are determined – so determined, in fact, that even the destruction of their newly built floating home by fire just weeks before the family were due to move on board didn't stop them from pursuing their dreams.

Green Credentials

A Clean Sweep

Green Credentials

The damage, probably caused by an electrical fault, would have put lesser souls off the idea. But after an extra ten months of dealing with the insurance company, manhandling building materials across jetties, and using floating cranes to reinstall a new staircase and windows, the family finally moved into their renovated home, renamed *Feniks* (Dutch for 'phoenix'). 'She really did rise from the ashes of the fire that nearly destroyed her,' Pieter observes, wryly. Looking back, he can now joke that the whole project was worthy of an episode of *Grand Designs*.

The second thing to know about the couple is that they are as passionate about a certain way of life on the water – and where their craft would be moored – as about the history or design of the boat itself. Located north of Amsterdam, the unique neighbourhood where *Feniks* now resides comprises thirty houseboats and is known as 'Schoonschip' – an echo of the Dutch expression *schoon schip maken*, which loosely translates as 'making a clean sweep', or 'cleaning things up'.

'Schoonschip began fifteen years ago as a private initiative,' Pieter says. 'It took many years of dreaming, planning, lobbying, setbacks and paperwork to finally get it off the ground, from getting the council to appoint a location to obtaining permits for the experimental sustainable platform. And this was even before we started the design process.'

The result is not only a beautiful, energy-neutral village of houseboats, but also a socially sustainable community. 'For me, this is the biggest achievement of Schoonschip,' he adds. 'The long development process has been a catalyst for strong community-building. We all know and care for each other, while maintaining plenty of personal space for all of the different personalities. The fact that we live on houseboats is key – on the water, you feel that you still have your privacy, even with others living so close by. Schoonschip is an example of a real community, not one of those synthesized versions that are too dogmatic or superficial.'

Feniks itself was designed by Pieter, along with John Kusters, and is shared by the family with their neighbour Irma. The combined houseboat is only 175 m² (1,884 sq ft), with 95 m² (1,023 sq ft) for Pieter and Stefanie and 80 m² (861 sq ft) for Irma.

'We have created an incredible quality of life, which was one of the goals of this project,' Pieter explains. 'I trained as an engineer, and the technical aspect is as important to me as the design. The staircase is built from 30 mm (1 in.)-thick Russian birch plywood, without using a single screw. It's quite an industrial material, and brings an authentic and layered aesthetic to the design. A good space combines complexity with clarity, and a good use of materials is logical and poetic at the same time. I think our boat is a good example of this.'

Pieter's golden rules for budgets

The first 80 per cent is money that needs to be spent anyway – on walls, windows, and so on.

The remaining 20 per cent is for the things that make a home wonderful, like materials and detailing. Most building projects will succumb to financial pressure, and it is this second part of the budget that tends to be sacrificed, even though the finishing touches are what bring the most joy to the end result.

Try flipping this approach and cut costs in the first 80 per cent, keeping the remainder intact. This can be achieved by building less square footage, or adding another storey a few years later.

Know your environmental footprint

Do a personal environmental-footprint scan for you and your family. People talk a lot about sustainability, but don't know enough about the effects of their own habits.

Since I no longer eat meat and live in an energy-neutral home, I wondered what the main areas of impact were in my life. It soon became clear that it was food transportation – so no more avocados from New Zealand.

The scan can be the tipping point that finally convinces you to change your behaviour, like getting a job closer to home, so you don't have to drive every day. For us, it was the catalyst to switch to an electric car-sharing initiative.

Opposite
Planting around the decking creates an outdoor room and blurs the boundaries between inside and out.

With its beautiful, light-filled rooms, it is easy to see how the combination of technical know-how and sharp design has transformed the family's home life. 'One of the best things about the boat is that it has so many places for retreat or hanging out,' he adds. 'I will drift to a preferred spot depending on the weather, time of day or my mood, but everywhere in the house has its own special quality.'

Pieter and Stefanie also wanted outside space, so a floating terrace was created to support a garden. 'We have a lot of green inside and out,' Pieter says. 'This is very important, and it is bliss to have this in the urban context of our boat. We have a pear tree, and it produced enough fruit to fill a couple of buckets last year. There are also berries, tomatoes and various vegetables growing in the garden and on the roof terrace. Around the boats, birds build their nests and swans and ducks set up their homes. The ducklings make a lot of noise! It has really been a multiplier of positivity, aesthetically and socially.'

Creating a floating garden

The garden is made from foam blocks, 1 × 1 m (3 × 3 ft), wrapped in sturdy netting and mesh to prevent crumbling, and knotted together with rope. This allows the garden to move with the waves of passing boats, absorbing shocks, and does away with the need for a rigid structure.

On top of each block is a layer of earth, 20 cm (8 in.) deep. Plant roots grip the netting, and grow down towards the water between the blocks. Part of the garden is set lower, level with the water, with a wooden frame and a simple, permeable floor. This is where we grow reeds, which help knit the structure together and do not need any care. They get all the nutrients they need from the canal water, which is brackish and slightly salty. In summer, the reeds grow very high, creating a green barrier between our terrace and the neighbours.

When choosing plants, take note of the wind, as not every species will thrive in windy conditions. Choose only those that are strong enough to survive the constant exposure to sun. Most of the plants just drink rainwater; the roots of the pear tree and the reeds are in saltwater, however, and grow like mad.

Opposite
The spiral staircase in plywood is a stunning focal feature in this modern houseboat.

Green Credentials

A Clean Sweep

Green Credentials

Above
A glimpse into the open-plan living area is framed by houseplants, an essential part of the decor.

Right
The tranquillity of the floating garden provides the perfect escape from city living.

Opposite
Floor-to-ceiling glazing in the dining area allows a wonderful panorama of the waterfront.

A Clean Sweep

Above
The office is clean and minimal;
the plywood is repeated in the
office bedroom.

Right
The bathroom is a compact
but usable space.

Opposite
This bright and cheerful bedroom
belongs to the couple's son,
and comes complete with a
swinging rope.

A Clean Sweep

Amazing Spaces
Reetainer, UK

Walking into a dusty industrial estate in East London some seven years ago, Max McMurdo wondered if he had just embarked on the perhaps maddest project of his life. Standing in front of a 12 × 2 m (40 × 8 ft) shipping container, rusted and dented, the full realization of what he had just done dawned on him. He had sold his beloved cottage in Bedford, some 48 km (30 miles) out of London, and was about to spend £2,000 on a metal shipping container to live in ... on the water.

Right
Rather than cladding the container in wood, Max made a feature of its industrial heritage.

Opposite
In summer, a reinforced concrete pontoon doubles as extra living space; the bi-fold doors open to allow full use of the decked area.

Amazing Spaces

Green Credentials

'It looked really small,' Max recollects now. And it was not only small, but also battered, having travelled thousands of miles across the globe and visibly wearing its years of service in the transport industry, with corrosion, scratches and dents everywhere. What had he done?

The journey to the East London industrial estate began, at least in part, with Max's late father, who had inspired his son to work hard and dream big, and left him with a boyhood ambition to be mortgage-free by the time he was forty. Now Max saw a way this could be realized. 'I had just finished renovating my cottage, and had added about £50,000 of value,' he says. 'I could be debt-free and on the water.'

As he found himself surveying the interior of the metal box, a shaft of sunlight streamed through the industrial doors and dust particles danced in the stale air. It was hard to imagine that this dark, rusting hulk would become a floating home on the River Ouse. But imagine he did: it was time to think outside the box and take on the challenge. 'I'd always dreamt of living by the water in a tiny home, so it was the perfect time,' he adds. He took the plunge.

Max certainly had a good idea of design and property challenges. After studying product design at Bournemouth University, he forged an exciting, if conventional, career as a car designer and teacher, and spent a fulfilling year working for Ford in Germany. But soon he began to notice how far behind the UK was in using reclaimed and discarded materials to create innovative designs, and started thinking about how the market could be better served.

Back home, he abandoned car design and began to restore, design and manufacture high-end furniture from waste destined for landfill. An appearance in 2007 on the BBC's *Dragon's Den* – in which budding entrepreneurs pitch for investors' money – enabled him to secure investment and upscale the company significantly. 'I went on to sell items, including my bathtub chairs, to businesses like the Body Shop for their stores around the world, and completed several installations for Google's head offices,' he says. 'I loved the playfulness and provocative nature of working with salvaged materials.'

Television soon came calling, and Max has made regular appearances on Channel 4's *George Clarke's Amazing Spaces* and *Kirstie's Fill Your House for Free*. 'Renovating a property is lovely,' he says, 'but building a home from scratch is an absolute dream come true. You can make it so personal and design it around your needs.'

It was this that feeling that fed into Max's ambition to convert the container into a home for a life on the water. This wasn't his first time converting a shipping container:

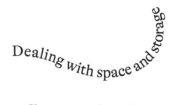

Dealing with space and storage

Clever storage is key to the success of my home, from a floating floor, 60 cm (2 ft) from the base, which allows me to hide the bath, white goods and wardrobes, to a dining table that rises from the floor via a scissor lift to create an eating area. When not in use, it drops back down to free up space in the living room.

The coolest part of the bedroom design is the hidden wardrobe: the full-sized bed divides in the middle and slides apart to reveal steps leading down into a large closet below.

I also wanted to install a full-sized suite in the bathroom. Rather than a boat toilet, there's a regular model and a rather clever shower/bath set up. The shower floor is made of a pebble-covered mesh that slides back to reveal a stainless-steel tub below, so just one drainage system is needed. The bathroom and kitchen share a sink, which called for a tilting tap that can be accessed from either space. It is made from a piece of aluminium scaffolding pole and a riveted brown leather belt, combining high-end design and reclaimed materials.

Opposite
An upcycled washing machine drum, used as a plant pot for an olive tree, and teapot bird feeder adorn the outside space.

Green Credentials

in 2012 he turned one into an office, which nestled comfortably at the bottom of his cottage garden. The following year he transformed two to make a single school classroom, which is still in use today. Building something that would survive on water, though, brought a whole set of new challenges. It sits on a reinforced concrete pontoon, bought secondhand, which provides extra outside decking and on sunny days doubles as a living space. But when the weather is bad, it's even more extreme on board.

'I can cope with rain, sun, snow, and even floods, but strong winds are not nice,' Max says. 'Everything creaks and groans, with items blowing everywhere, and the smaller boats rock terribly. I'm always tinkering and improving. Designers are never happy. I've fitted a hot tub under the decking, and this year solar panels to the roof. I'm also planning to remove the oil-fuelled Rayburn and fit infrared heating in the ceiling, which is more comfortable and better for the planet because of its low energy consumption.'

Would he make a move to living back on the land? 'I can't see ever wanting to move back, no,' Max concludes. 'I'm mortgage-free, have minimal overheads, am at one with nature and know that I have a very small footprint on the planet.' Both he and the East London shipping container have come a long way.

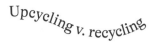

Upcycling v. recycling

The term 'upcycling' should focus as much on the 'up' as on the recycling part of the process. Whereas recycling is about returning an object to its original properties, upcycling adds value – through innovative design, imagination and hand-work – to make it more desirable. It was one thing; now it's a better thing.

Upcycling is not difficult. It's about expressing your creativity and being brave. If you are new to it, try working on something like a dining chair at first. With some stripping, sanding, painting and upholstery, it is amazing what can be achieved.

In my own home, I've upcycled nearly everything. It's my signature, if you like – from the jelly-mould pendant lamps to the bicycle-seat stools and illuminated washing-machine side table.

Left
In the compact bathroom, the pebbled mesh floor slides back to reveal a full-sized bath below.

Opposite
Max and a friend enjoy a morning coffee on board *Reetainer*.

Amazing Spaces

Green Credentials

Above
A retractable table beneath the rug rises up from the floor to create an eating area, and drops back down when not in use.

Right
The tilting tap can be accessed from the kitchen or the bathroom by simply turning it on its axis.

Opposite
Bar stools made from tractor seats and scaffolding poles add a dash of industrial chic.

Amazing Spaces

Above
The bed frame is also made from scaffolding poles, and the bedside lamp from a sweets jar.

Left
A suitcase doubles as a side table for extra storage.

Opposite
The tilting tap, seen on the bathroom side.

Green Credentials

Amazing Spaces

Plug & Play
Altar, Brazil

'Tiny house', 'off-grid', 'eco': three buzzwords or phrases that increasingly capture the zeitgeist. But what about a tiny, off-grid, eco-house that floats? A thoughtfully designed, compact and sustainable contemporary home for living on the water? That's enough buzz to put a beehive out of business.

Right
Sunset over the Jaguariúna reservoir – just one of the incredible natural beauties that set the screen for *Altar's* mooring place.

Overleaf
Floor-to-ceiling windows create a generous viewing gallery; in the evenings, the exterior wall doubles up as a cinema screen.

Green Credentials

This was the dream for Rodrigo Martins and his family, along with two friends, Renata and Marcelo – a dream that is now an alluring 64 m² (689 sq ft) reality called *Altar*, anchored on the tranquil waters of the Jaguariúna reservoir in the foothills of the Mantiqueira mountain range, some two hours north of São Paulo in Brazil.

'We created *Altar* with the intention of offering people, and ourselves, a very different place to live,' Rodrigo explains. 'I didn't have any previous marine experience – no one in my family did – but I did have a desire to create something sustainable and off-grid, which could adapt to any setting. It was Marcelo, one of my oldest friends, who came up with the notion of building a house on the water. I found the idea incredible, so we worked together to make it happen.'

The breakthrough came when they teamed up with the Brazilian sustainable prefab manufacturer sysHaus to use its net-zero LilliHaus system, which in this aquatic incarnation has been dubbed a 'Water LilliHaus'. The diminutive 38 m² (410 sq ft) structure is produced from 100 per cent recyclable materials, including refurbished hardwoods. Alongside the airy, open-plan kitchen/dining/living space is a stylish bathroom and a double bedroom with floor-to-ceiling windows, affording the rare opportunity to fall asleep while looking at one landscape, and waking up to a completely different view, thanks to the wind-propelled drift of the houseboat around its anchor point.

Altar is self-sufficient for energy and water. Electricity is generated by rooftop solar panels, complemented by energy-efficient lighting and strategically sited openings in the floor and ceiling for natural ventilation, while advanced water-treatment systems provide clean drinking water and purify all waste before it is returned safely to the environment. Being completely self-contained, the boat could be located anywhere, so it took only a small leap of imagination to have it delivered, completely finished, to the reservoir.

Plug & Play

Mounted on a wooden wraparound deck atop a catamaran, *Altar* can sail at a stately maximum speed of four knots – just enough to manoeuvre into pool position, drop anchor and simply be – and rest. That generous deck is one of Rodrigo's favourite features. Adding 26 m² (280 sq ft) of living space to the house, it's also the perfect place to sit, read and reflect, enjoy an al fresco movie after dark or, when adventure beckons, dive from into the clear, clean water.

Are there any downsides to this off-grid idyll? Rodrigo pauses for a moment. 'If there has to be a disadvantage, it would be crossing the reservoir by dinghy to reach the boat in bad weather,' he admits. 'The upside is that once everyone is inside, you can sit around the fire and enjoy the exuberance of nature.'

And that is key to his philosophy: letting go of the 24/7 relationship with your mobile phone and reconnecting with yourself, those you love and the natural world. 'The first time we stayed on the boat, we went through several hours of what felt like agony, because there was no internet access or phone signal,' he says. 'It made us realize just how addicted we were to being online. After two or three hours of worrying about what we were going to do with the children, we all started to switch off, kids included, and appreciate the views and the feeling of being disconnected. *Altar* is a lesson in how you can enjoy everything that nature has to offer, how to recycle and live a greener life. We don't live on board permanently – it's for weekends and holidays, and we rent it out at other times – but the experiences we've had in our floating house have made it pretty certain that our next adventure is to get a sailboat and travel around the world.'

Somehow, that's not too surprising.

The pleasure of entertaining

One unexpected bonus that we discovered when we bought *Altar* is that it is the perfect setting for creating memories. The time we spend here with family and friends is priceless. When you are floating in a place of such incredible beauty, with the mountains as a backdrop and no internet, you can fully connect with each other and with your surroundings.

We are careful to keep the numbers down, both to create a more intimate gathering and because – unlike entertaining at home, where you can invite as many guests as you wish – we have to be mindful of capacity. But we don't mind, it just gives us an excuse to do it all again another day.

The days spent socializing often drift into the evening. At sunset, we lie on the deckchairs, wrapped up in blankets, and watch a movie on the outdoor cinema screen. It's just like something out of a film.

Green Credentials

Above
The interior was made from
100 per cent recyclable
materials, including refurbished
hardwoods.

Right
The only enclosed room is the
bathroom; a skylight cut into the
ceiling turns it into a light and
airy space.

Opposite
The wood-burning stove is a
cosy and attractive source
of heating throughout winter.

Plug & Play

Left
Room with a view: the foothills of the Mantiqueira mountains provide a stunning backdrop.

Below
The master bedroom: there can be few better places from which to greet the day.

Opposite
A neat, functional kitchen with a pared-back feel complements the interior design.

Overleaf
According to owner Rodrigo, *Altar* provides 'a lesson for life: enjoy everything that nature has to offer.'

Green Credentials

Plug & Play

Green Credentials

Plug & Play

Green Credentials

Afloat in the Delta
Mini, Argentina

Life-changing ideas often take months, or years, to take shape. Not in Anibal Guiser Gleyzer's case, however: he can remember the exact place and time he took his first step on the path towards a very different life.

Right
Shoes lined up, ready for any occasion.

Opposite
Owner Anibal's floating home *Mini* was inspired by South American wood-carrying barges.

Overleaf
The houseboat blends in harmoniously with its surroundings, becoming part of nature, instead of fighting it.

Afloat in the Delta

'We need to go back thirty years, to the town of San Pedro in Buenos Aires province,' he says. 'I had reached a point where I realized that nothing matters if you're not doing what you want. At that moment, I decided to buy a sailboat, restore it, and explore the beautiful delta of the Paraná and Uruguay rivers.'

This was when Anibal's beloved sailboat *El Terrible* came into his life, but it was only when a business venture went disastrously wrong, leaving him with massive debts, that his masterplan finally got the kickstart it needed.

'I had to sell my house in Buenos Aires, but rather than move into a tiny apartment, I decided to find some land in the delta, build a house and live next to my sailboat,' he says. 'Then I got the idea of doing something more collective, perhaps with friends – of starting a venture that could also be a business. Until then, I had always thought of houses in the delta as being on stilts set into the ground. I began to realize that the entire region has been at the mercy of the waters for thousands of years – the skeleton of a whale was found in a neighbour's garden – and that if we want to inhabit the territory of the waters, the best thing to do is to float. Out of that came the idea of making an ecological community designed specially for floating houses: Econáutico Hipocampo.'

How to live in the moment

When I cut the grass with my scythe or pick leaves for a salad, I am fully in the present. It's the same with swimming, kayaking or sailing. All these things can lead to meditation, without having to be motionless in the lotus position for half an hour. The key is not to think – or think too much – and to disassociate yourself from the noise of the world.

One of the tenets of Buddhism is to be the change you want to see in the world. It is one of the best commitments we can make. Another is that your first mission is to be happy, so you can give the best of yourself to the world. Working and living on the water allows you to live these principles, far more so than living on land.

Green Credentials

Afloat in the Delta

Below and opposite
The interior is marked by clean,
simple lines and a robust
structure.

Predictably, perhaps, Anibal's growing neighbourhood bears little resemblance to the kind of gated communities that are springing up in many modern cities. 'That model is very successful commercially, but extremely destructive in ecological terms,' he notes. 'No one who is interested in protecting the natural world would think of installing such a place in a wild habitat. Projects with the primary goal of maximizing profits not only cause pollution and waste, but also lead to the disappearance of everything that is natural. The challenge is to generate more profitable permaculture ventures than gated communities, so that developers can take this new model and make money without causing damage. That is the difference between "urbanize" and "humanize".'

Focus on real beauty

Our thoughtless consumerism of things we don't really need is destroying the planet.

I have had the same car for thirty-eight years. It is a VW Beetle that left the factory in December 1957 and is about to turn sixty-five years old. But it's far from finished. At some point, I'll run it on hydrogen or convert it to electric or use clean fuel made from recycled plastic waste.

Each new car represents a considerable environmental footprint – a cost to the planet. The future is in restoring and updating your transport – car, boat, whatever – instead of buying something new every three years.

When Anibal set out to design the houses for Econáutico Hipocampo, it felt important that they represent the culture of the region. The problem was that all the houses in the Tigre Delta – the area of the estuary that leads to the sea – were built in a European style. So what should a typical house look like? 'I discovered that there is something that is omnipresent from Paraguay to El Plata, and that is the flat-hulled barge that transports wood through the rivers and streams of the delta,' he says.

'From its shape, I made the first drawing of a houseboat,' he continues. 'The final design is based on that drawing, and work began in 2013. It is a two-storey house with a covered area of 52 m² (560 sq ft), and sits on a ferrocement hull. It was the first to be built in the complex, and the closest thing to eco-friendly I could get at the time. None of the materials used to build it were ecologically viable, so I spent the next ten years researching and experimenting with different forms of bioconstruction. Eventually I developed a new building method called Natural10, which uses materials with a healthy ecological footprint and combines ancient construction techniques with an assembly process that doesn't require specialized builders. The construction has been a path of discovery: one great success was the choice of ferrocement as the material for the floats in our houses. It evolved into a modular system, which was developed by one of our neighbours.'

Has it all been worth it? Anibal is in no doubt. 'In winter, we enjoy the salamander fire. In summer, it is beautiful to swim and row in the canal. Autumn dazzles us with its colour palette, and in the spring we admire the birds. There are moments when nature engulfs us completely, when there are storms and great floods. My crush on Econáutico Hipocampo continues to grow.'

Afloat in the Delta

Above
Anibal's original plan was to build on land by the delta, but the appeal of a fully floating home soon took over.

Right
Nature on the doorstep.

Opposite
Work on the houseboat began in 2013; it was the first to be built in what is now a thriving water-borne community.

Green Credentials

Afloat in the Delta

Creating an Urban Retreat

The appeal of water-borne urban communities everywhere lies in the special combination of light, economy and the novelty of living on the water, surrounded by the buzz of the city. What could be finer?

A Community on the Water
Boat With No Name, USA

Photographer Philip Newton hadn't looked at many floating homes before deciding to buy this one on Lake Union in Seattle, Washington. In truth, he hadn't really thought about making a life on the water at all. He knew about the community of houseboats in the city, but had never imagined being part of it.

Left
Potted plants adorn the pontoon walkways that link this floating community.

Opposite
Philip Newton makes his way across the water on *Little Red*.

Overleaf
Life on the waters of Lake Union, right in the heart of Seattle, is a surprisingly rural experience.

Creating an Urban Retreat

A Community on the Water

Creating an Urban Retreat

A Community on the Water

Philip traces his passion for the water to growing up on Vancouver Island in British Columbia, on the western edge of Canada – 'a stone's throw from the ocean' – and making regular visits to his grandparents' waterfront property.

'When I saw this floating home,' he says, 'I knew immediately that this was where I wanted to live. Not only were the bones of the house perfect, but it also had a big dock and a sailboat already moored there. It brought those far-off memories flooding back.'

Every craft tells a story, but some yield more clues as to their origins than others. Philip's house didn't even have a formal name. 'It is difficult to date the first floating homes, because there are no records as they were never official,' he says. 'The community was peopled by heretics, social and economic misfits, criminals and blue-collar workers who couldn't find anywhere else to live, so records are few and far between. Floating homes were on the margins, and used as escapes as much as residences.'

Above
Wooden shingles were used to clad the exterior; they are natural insulators, as well as being water- and rot-resistant.

Above right
The water-borne homes on the lake have few historical records.

Opposite
Once home to 'heretics and misfits', the neighbourhood is now a friendly community.

Creating an Urban Retreat

The community spirit is a big part of what I like here. We regularly get together to work on the infrastructure, make decisions, share food and drink, and lend or borrow tools and books. It's like living in a small village.

Living on the water has all of the conveniences of living on land. It is just as dry, too – unless, of course, you fall in. I have lost lots of tools, phones and glasses to the bottom of the lake.

Entertaining is a big part of having a house on the water. Everyone wants to visit, and on the Fourth of July you can drift from one party to the next.

It is rumoured that his boat was once home to a communist printing press. 'As to how old it is,' Philip adds, 'my only clue is a newspaper from 1931 that I found in the walls when doing some renovation.' A glance at the vessel's lines suggests an age of at least ninety years, possibly more, so the newspaper is as good a clue as any. As with much historical research, what is to hand becomes what is useful.

Before Philip bought the boat in 2011, its owner was a writer who used it as his creative base. Creature comforts were few and far between: 'There was no real kitchen,' he says. 'A Murphy bed was in the bedroom, but otherwise it was empty.'

So there was a good deal of work to do, but as importantly, this also meant a near-blank canvas. Philip pulled in an architect friend, Prentis Hale, and the pair set about creating the cool, restrained, intelligently composed craft you see here. The key to the design was not to rush into any work without a period of acclimatization. 'I took down a few walls to open up the space, and then pretty much camped out,' he says. 'I learned how the

A Community on the Water

Philip's tips for a simpler lifestyle

In Seattle, local produce is available by boat, with a number of accessible shops or farmer's markets. If there isn't public mooring, I create my own on the shore or borrow from the docks around the waterway. Just ask, be polite and leave a bottle of wine.

For me, finding inspiration is about dropping everything and getting in the water. Sometimes I put my wetsuit on and just float on my back, looking at the sky. Nothing to do other than float, no particular destination or activity required.

Being clever about how you store and organize is a wonderful game. I go to the local boat show just to see how creative one can be when living in confined quarters.

light and space worked. We could have put the kitchen, bedroom or living room in any number of different configurations, but I wanted to see how the light fell, and how the boat as a whole felt over different seasons and in changing weather conditions.'

The result is that no singular style dominates – 'mid-century modern-meets-rustic cabin, maybe?' Philip muses – but there is also inspiration from the *minka*, a traditional Japanese housing style, in the mix, too, so the choice of furniture and layout had to work harmoniously with the bones of the interior. A 'spend, spend, spend' approach would very likely have missed much of the subtlety that Philip and Prentis have achieved.

Having downsized from a 280 m² (3,000 sq ft) house to an 85 m² (900 sq ft) floating home, Philip pared down his belongings to only those that were personal and precious to him. Following the usual mantras of interior-boat design was never going to be on the cards, and the oft-taken route of inserting extra storage held no appeal. 'I refused to get an outside storage space, and found I delighted in living with less stuff,' he says.

Creating an Urban Retreat

'Less stuff' doesn't mean second-rate, however. The focus from the start was on upcycling, good husbandry and a robust aesthetic that chimes perfectly with the boat's long, if largely unknown, history. 'Sourcing was from surplus and recycled warehouses, Craig's List, thrift stores and things I found on the street,' he adds. 'Even the lumber used for the kitchen cabinets was construction-grade plywood, which – with sanding and finishing – has been transformed into something beautiful.'

While the pared-down approach works for the interior, the outside was at one stage in danger of becoming something of a water-borne parking area. 'Since moving onto the water, I collected and hoarded anything that could float: canoe, kayak, sailboat, rowing shell, paddleboards, inflated inner tube,' Philip confesses. 'I have since edited the collection down and now just have *Little Red*, a red rubber dinghy with an outboard. I use it regularly for grocery shopping, dining out, going to the bar, movies, and entertaining myself and others. My preference is always to do it by boat whenever possible.'

Above
No single style dominates the interior, allowing the design to follow what 'works with the bones' of the boat.

Opposite
The plywood kitchen is both beautiful and hardwearing.

A Community on the Water

Left
Philip sums up his interior-design style as 'mid-century modern-meets-rustic cabin'.

Below
Space may be tight, but the kitchen area is thoroughly practical, with room for everything he needs.

Opposite
Philip's focus from the beginning was on upcycling and living happily with less.

Creating an Urban Retreat

A Community on the Water

Above
The sense of solitude in a busy
city creates a peaceful
environment for Philip's studio.

Opposite
A cool, restrained craft:
according to Philip, 'less'
doesn't mean 'second rate'.

Downsides? According to Philip, those only amount to living in such close quarters with one's neighbours: 'You find your favourite people, and then just be cordial to the rest.'

For this professional photographer, the upsides win out by a considerable margin. 'I was instantly attracted to the light,' he says. 'I still am, plus the space and the atmosphere – not only of the house itself, but also of the surrounding aquatic landscape. Although Lake Union is situated in the very heart of Seattle, it provides both wide open space and solitude in this dense urban setting.'

Add in the great blue herons fishing off the dock, or the beavers swimming under and around the boat, and you can understand how this convert to water-borne living sees no reason to move off the boat with no name any time soon.

A Community on the Water

French Navy
Le Cid, France

There is an old transport barge moored on the Seine in Paris, between the Pont Alexandre III and Pont de la Concorde. It is called *Le Cid* and has been there since 1980, but nobody is quite sure now how she got there.

Creating an Urban Retreat

Above
Mooring lines and the other detritus of boat life are a far cry from Agnès's career in fashion.

Opposite
There can be few more iconic views than the one *Le Cid* enjoys from her mooring in central Paris.

Overleaf
Large skylights fill the barge with natural light; the wood-burner is a secondary source of heat.

French Navy

Creating an Urban Retreat

What is known is fascinating: the barge – known at birth as Xerxes V – was built in 1930 in Mainz, Germany, and immediately handed over to France as part of the post-First World War reparations demanded by the Treaty of Versailles. From there, she made its way to Bordeaux, where she began her unglamorous life as a workhorse in the city's teeming port and shipyards.

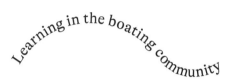

Learning in the boating community

My neighbours soon discovered I worked in fashion. I learned by listening, then doing. I soon realized there are two kinds of boaters: those who see difficulties and leave after a few years, and those who see past the problems and stay forever.

The harbour committee needed a secretary general, and a neighbour asked if I wanted to join. I am the second woman to join the committee, which until then was 80 per cent men. I've learned a lot about boating systems, working with the harbour authorities and dealing with watery challenges.

When planning began for the 2024 Paris Olympics, it was unclear if we would be allowed to stay. We wrote many emails and letters pointing out that our boats could provide opportunities for the water-based events.

The harbour is listed as a UNESCO World Heritage site, along with the Pont Alexandre III and the Eiffel Tower. Our boats are a part of Paris and its history. For the moment, the Games will go ahead with our cooperation. It shows not only that boating communities often have to fight for their security of tenure, but also that it is worth defending.

A decade later, Germany took the barge back. When France fell in 1940, Bordeaux became a vital haven for Hitler's Atlantic operations and *Xerxes V* went to work for the enemy. She was moved up the coast to St Nazaire to service the German submarine flotillas, and that's where she was in 1945 when an Allied bombardment battered the port area into submission – causing disastrous damage to the boat in the process.

Refloated and returned to Bordeaux after the war, *Xerxes V* found a new peacetime role working for a French oil company, which in 1954 was bought by British Petroleum, who proudly renamed the wounded old warhorse *BP Toulouse*. After a few decades of honourable hard labour,

BP Toulouse was pensioned off, excused further heavy-lifting duties, and turned into a floating home in 1980 with yet another name, this time inspired by the most popular historical epic of the time: *Le Cid*. And this is where the story goes a little foggy.

Le Cid was sold again in 1980, but by this time had somehow completed her own epic voyage to Paris, having travelled 2,600 km (1,600 miles) along the canals and western seaboard of France since her launch half a century earlier. And there she sat for another forty years until 2018, when she became the beloved home of Agnès Combes Bernageau, her two children and their French bulldog.

As this book shows, there is no such thing as a 'typical' boat owner, but Agnès is one of the more surprising. As a senior executive at a renowned French luxury fashion brand, she might be expected to live in one of Paris's more colourful or sought-after *quartiers* – Montmartre perhaps, or Le Marais – but that's not her style. 'I was bored with the rather impersonal life of conventional Paris,' she says. 'It was time for a change, and it only took me half an hour on the internet to find *Le Cid* and fall in love.'

One of the most appealing things about Agnès's new life is not being stuck in one place. 'That's the meaning of water and rivers: the possibility of leaving whenever you want,' she says. 'I moved from my cosy flat to my beloved boat on a gut feeling. One of my best life choices ever! I knew it would bring some changes, but didn't expect my life to blossom in such a way. A boat gives space for that.'

Agnès thinks for a moment. 'I have gained a more open mind and an open heart, as well as a community life and support system, and new friendships with a common mindset of freedom,' she continues. 'I also gained the ability to be the real me, all the time. I love to learn, and you do a lot of learning on boats – from moorings to all the technical stuff that I knew nothing about. I gained muscle strength and bruises and pride. And when an orphaned student offered to help out in the wheelhouse for free, I gained an adopted son.'

French Navy

What did Agnès lose? 'I lost my marriage,' she says with brutal honesty. 'It didn't survive the community life, the harbour spirit and a new addition to the family. That's the way it is. We were growing in opposite directions after ten years on the same path.'

And what do her neighbours make of her glamorous working life? 'At first, I didn't talk about my job with them, or about living on a boat when I met new people,' Agnès says. But it is the paradox of her water-borne life that holds the most appeal. 'The fact that I can be tightening a mooring line early in the morning, then grabbing my professional clothes and heading into the office is fascinating for some people,' she adds.

If there is a cliché emerging of an elegant Parisian lady holding high heels in her hand, jumping off the boat for the day and returning in the evening to enjoy the sunset with a glass of champagne, it is very much true.

'You just replace your high heels with Doc Martens and champagne with Spritz,' Agnès says. 'And don't forget the river floods in winter – then you go into the office in waders. More paradox, more fun.'

Creating an Urban Retreat

Below
Agnès moved onto the barge on the strength of a 'gut feeling', gaining, she says, 'a more open mind and an open heart'.

Opposite
Cool, clean lines mark out *Le Cid*'s interior, which boasts more living space than many small flats.

French Navy

Right
Boat life appealed to Agnès
for the freedom, as well as
'all the technical stuff' that
running a vessel involves.

Below, left and right
As befitting a boat that
moves on a regular basis,
the wheelhouse is smart
but functional.

Opposite
Open-plan living, flooded with
light: *Le Cid* has come a long
way from her former working
life in Bordeaux.

Creating an Urban Retreat

French Navy

Creating an Urban Retreat

Right
If these walls could talk:
Le Cid worked the canals
of southern France before
making the long trip to Paris.

Below
A log store is tucked into the
stairwell, watched over by the
family's French bulldog.

Opposite
Employing her fashion-
professional's eye, Agnès has
created a cool but restrained
interior design throughout.

French Navy

For most of the boat-dwellers featured within these pages, the idea of living on the water arose after seeing a beautiful vessel moored in a tranquil spot and deciding to buy it. Not Sarah Mittler and Marco Eckert, who made their dream come true the hard way: by deciding to live on the water in their hometown of Wiesbaden, Germany. So far, so good – except that the town isn't actually on the water, and, as Sarah points out, not many places in central Germany are.

Industrial Luxury
Lisbeth, Germany

Creating an Urban Retreat

This page
The urban vista of Wiesbaden
provides a beautiful backdrop to
Sarah and Marco's floating home.

Opposite
A ladder gives access to the sun
deck at the top of the boat.

Industrial Luxury

Above
Light floods into the open
kitchen, which reflects the
couple's ambition for an
industrial, minimalist design.

Opposite left
Open shelving makes the kitchen
feel wider, and is a simple and
stylish way to display glassware.

Opposite right
Sarah, Marco and their friends
often take to the water on
paddleboards.

'There are a few rivers and a couple of small lakes,' she adds, 'but it is nearly impossible to find a home next to the water that doesn't cost billions of Euros. So we decided not to live near the water, after all. We would live on it instead.'

What followed next will be horribly familiar to every member of the boat community the world over: the endless quest for the right vessel and the right place to put it.

'We applied for moorings at so many marinas, in so many cities within 150 km (93 miles) of our home, and talked to so many boat-builders in so many shipyards, from the Netherlands to Poland,' Marco says. 'In the end, we found the perfect berth in Frankfurt, only 30 km (19 miles) from Wiesbaden, and after looking at dozens of boats, we decided that the first houseboat we ever Googled was perfect. It was small, but when Sarah first moved in with me, she reduced her living space from 300 to 80 m^2 (3,230 to 860 sq ft), and we realized we didn't need much room. Home is not a space, it's a feeling.'

Living with curious neighbours

Living in a houseboat with huge windows in the middle of the city means living in a goldfish bowl. Almost every pedestrian, cyclist or passerby stops to take photos and ask questions. What is it like living on a boat? How long have you been here?

But we don't mind, and are always happy and willing to help those who are thinking about following a similar way of life in Germany. We still have fun being pioneers in our country.

All problems solved? Not quite – in fact, not even near. The couple's future home, quickly christened *Lisbeth* in honour of Sarah's much-loved and missed grandmother, was an abandoned, barely started project when they bought her in 2019. 'Nobody had ever lived on the boat,' says Sarah. 'Our job was to bring her to life.'

First, however, they had to bring *Lisbeth* from Berlin to Frankfurt. 'The original plan was to move her by land,' Marco explains. 'That was a huge challenge, because she is 18 m (59 ft) long and 6 m (20 ft) wide. It required a heavy loader, at least four escort vehicles and endless permits, then two giant cranes in Berlin and two more in Frankfurt. And then five days before the operation was due to start, a year-long building project began at the Frankfurt marina. It would have been impossible to gain access to our mooring by land.'

On to Plan B: loading *Lisbeth* onto a transporter and sailing her to Frankfurt. No problem, except for the lifting operation

What we've learned so far

First of all, the weather has a much bigger impact on water than on land. You have an immediate connection to storms, the wind and the waves. It's impressive to watch a blizzard from the water; the rain seems to come from above and below.

Secondly, you have to live self-sufficiently. There is no water connection on the canal, so we use a water tank.

And finally, with 21 tons of weight, we always have to be mindful of the overall weight distribution. Last summer, we put a jacuzzi on the terrace, which caused the boat to tilt. A counterweight was needed to rebalance it.

that resulted in *Lisbeth*'s side being ripped off even before they got out of Berlin, and the fact that the summer of 2019 in Germany was so hot that for months there wasn't enough water in the Rhine to float the boat. Then Coronavirus hit, leading to staff shortages among the river workers and endless delays at the many locks.

Eleven months, twenty-four days and 1,000 km (620 miles) later, *Lisbeth* finally arrived at her new home in Frankfurt – within 300 m (980 ft) of it, anyway. 'The outboard motor broke down and we were shipwrecked within sight of our mooring,' Marco says. 'Can you imagine how embarrassing it was to be towed the last few metres by a very small motor boat?'

The perils of the journey – and mortification of the arrival – were soon overtaken by the more enjoyable challenge of designing the interior and exterior spaces, as well as building the outside decking via the unusual method of standing on a paddleboard.

Creating an Urban Retreat

'We are typical self-builders,' Marco says. 'We wanted an exclusive but industrial, unfinished style, a clean and minimalist design. Our role model was Floating Dutch Design (FLODD). The principle is that there is no difference between furnishings on a boat and in a "normal" house, so that you don't feel you are missing anything. You wouldn't normally expect luxury on the water, but you notice that it is everywhere. The trick is that you shouldn't see it directly, and focus instead on being surrounded by nature, rather than luxurious furniture.'

Sarah adds: 'We love the morning, when the sunlight reflects on the water and streams through the windows, then making a cup of coffee, walking onto the floating terrace and enjoying the view. In the evening, our after-work celebration is a sundowner on the roof terrace. Every day is different. Drinking a glass of wine and talking to each other, watching the sun set over the Frankfurt skyline and being thankful we've had the opportunity to enjoy this way of life.'

At Home on a Super Yacht
Bella Coola, China

Nine years ago, Chrissy Carini and Danny Freer – both high-school teachers – left their home in East London to work in China, eventually finding jobs in Hong Kong. At first, they lived like so many of the residents in one of the world's most urbanized areas, in a tiny rented flat. Then, in 2021, came a once-in-a-lifetime opportunity to jump ship.

Left
In keeping with the couple's design preferences, objects and patterns from the 1960s and '70s are slowly being introduced.

Opposite
Hong Kong provides the stunning backdrop for the couple's spacious, water-borne home.

Overleaf
An L-shaped sofa separates the open-plan living and dining areas, and provides plenty of seating for dogs and people.

Creating an Urban Retreat

At Home on a Super Yacht

Creating an Urban Retreat

Today their home is *Bella Coola*, a 230 m² (2,500 sq ft) yacht with five decks and three gardens, which they share with six dogs – including thirteen-year-old Nikolai, who moved with them from London, and five rescue animals. 'I'm sure we look like crazy people,' Chrissy laughs, 'but we just love dogs. The dog-rescue people know us because we've got all this room and we don't have kids, so we can take in the really bad cases that no one will adopt – the ones with behavioural issues and disabilities like Reggie, a two-and-a-half-legged Pomeranian who walks on his hind legs, or Derpington, our blind chihuahua.'

Making a garden on board

We became obsessed with growing our own herbs and vegetables, but cultivating a garden on a boat requires planning and dedication, with challenges that are unique to life afloat – salty air and potential typhoons being just two of them.

Initially, seedlings need to be protected as much as possible, so we grow plants like chives, tomatoes, chillies and mint under a canopy, where they are protected from the elements and have less sun exposure. At the moment, we have thirteen mango trees we've grown from seed.

There are no natural predators, like geckos or spiders, when bugs attack. We used to get plants from the flower market, and a few times I brought in pests that took a whole crop out. And, of course, pollination is a problem. It's a case of trial and error; sending a few plants to their watery grave is not uncommon.

What Chrissy does find crazy is that two 'ordinary' schoolteachers like themselves could end up living in so glamorous a home. Do people assume they are rich? She's quick to scotch that idea. 'We're not rich,' she says, crisply. 'We just had good timing and took a huge risk. *Bella Coola* would have cost £700,000, new, in 2008. She was a custom-build – the hull was made in China, and the interiors customized at the shipyard in Hong Kong. There are about twenty boats of this design around, and no two interior layouts are the same.'

At Home on a Super Yacht

Chrissy adds: 'The only reason we have *Bella Coola* is because an economic downturn led to some people moving away. We had some savings and had been thinking about buying a flat in Bangkok, but then we found out about boats like this being sold cheaply. We picked her up for £170,000, a fraction of the original value, and the bank wrote off the rest.'

While it all sounds glamorous compared to life in Ilford, living on board is not that straightforward. For a start, in Hong Kong you are allowed to 'stay' on a boat, but not live in it as your primary home. It's the type of legal fudge that works fine, as long as you don't rock the, well, boat. Then there's the small matter of being moored in a public typhoon shelter, which they could be kicked out of at any time.

Retro-futuristic design

We still have a long way to go before we're happy with the interior design, but we've begun to make headway and are introducing an aesthetic that's more to our taste: retro-futurism.

We like 1960s and '70s vibes – visions of the future from the past – so we're drawn to touches of space-age design and stylistic combinations of old-fashioned retro with futuristic technology.

The previous owners were South African, and when we moved on board, a rather large coffee table decorated with the South African flag dominated the living room. There were a lot of non-native hardwood accessories and internal details that had been incorporated into the interior. We are slowly replacing these, but the kitchen is going to be a big job.

The upside is living cheaply but in some style, bang in the middle of the fourth most densely populated place on the planet. 'We get a lot of wildlife, including massive jellyfish, which is amazing in such highly polluted water,' Chrissy says. 'Even in a typhoon, when the sea is flying all around you, *Bella Coola* remains perfectly still because we're in the shelter – although I do have to bring the plants inside.'

Caring for rescue dogs

There is no one way to care for our rescue dogs, as they each have different needs.

Our dogs have seen some bad times. Reggie, our Pomeranian, had to have one of his front legs amputated, and the other cannot bear any weight. But after months of intensive care and love, he is now socializing with humans again and can be seen riding around in the *sampan* (water taxi) when he's not trotting around the boat on his hind legs.

Two of our dogs have spinal problems, two were severely neglected, one is blind and another is deaf. But after years of trauma, they now have access to fresh air, space and lots of attention. This is magical for them, and we hope they love it.

After being on board for eighteen months, the couple still have a lot of work to do. 'The boat needs investment and updating – the kitchen irritates me, and the bathrooms are gross,' she adds. 'We're trying to fix her up, bit by bit, as and when we can afford it. We have plans to make her solar-powered, but so far it's been mostly plumbing, electrics and wood restoration. Right now, we're stopping the leaks, which involves grinding off the fibreglass and recoating it – a very long, nasty job.'

And what are the longterm plans for, as Chrissy so aptly calls her, *TBC*? 'We've been in Hong Kong for nine years, and I didn't think I'd ever leave, but a lot can change quickly in these wild times,' she muses. 'Eventually, we'd love to take her to Thailand. We wouldn't even have to worry about driving her there – they just pop boats like ours onto a container ship with a crane. She has a diesel engine, but she isn't independent of power, so she's not a pleasure cruiser. Sailing her is a pain – you have to hire a captain and your refrigerator stops working!'

Creating an Urban Retreat

At Home on a Super Yacht

Creating an Urban Retreat

Above
The boat bristles with neat design touches throughout.

Right
Bella Coola was custom-made, but Sarah and Marco were able to buy her for a fraction of the original price.

Opposite
There is plenty of space for the couple's large and much-loved family of rescue dogs.

On p. 85
Potted plants provide a supply of fresh herbs and vegetables, and are brought inside during typhoon season.

At Home on a Super Yacht

Creating an Urban Retreat

Left
Inside, the emphasis is on comfort and quirky details.

Below
Plans for the future include a possible trip to Thailand. For the moment, however, Hong Kong suits the couple just fine.

Opposite
The towering cityscape, seen from one of the boat's five decks.

At Home on a Super Yacht

Moored up, *Bella Coola* makes a striking first impression.

Creating an Urban Retreat

At Home on a Super Yacht

The Nomadic Lifestyle

If the journey is the thing, these boats offer the perfect form of travel. From a yellow converted rescue craft to a sleek modernist vessel built up from a shell, meet the water-based homes that will go wherever the mood takes you.

Seventy Degrees North
Stødig, Norway

The Nomadic Lifestyle

Life on their converted lifeboat *Stødig* (Norwegian for 'steady') has been far from uneventful for architects Guylee Simmonds and David Schnabel, with the challenges faced in refitting her and then sailing her some 5,000 km (over 3,100 miles) pushing them well out of their comfort zones. *Stødig* had already spent most of her working life as a rescue boat in Scotland. For her new owners, the initial outlay required was modest – some £7,000 – and they liked that she was rugged, durable and safe, as well as spacious. Once the boat was transported by road from Scotland down to East Sussex, they set about making her ready for the trip of a lifetime.

Right
On Norway's national day, Guylee takes the not-so-traditional route of celebrating with a swim.

Opposite
Stødig in her natural environment: the stunning waterways of northern Europe.

Seventy Degrees North

Departing from the UK, Guylee and David sailed to Europe and then up and into the Norwegian Arctic. The aim was to have a slow adventure, one that would be 'a slingshot into a new life'. Having met at university, they always knew they would do something different. 'It started off as hiking,' Guylee remembers. 'We were constantly talking about what the next thing would be. That's how the idea of this voyage came about.'

Stødig needed a full internal refit, along with the addition of enough equipment to make her independent and reliable. The couple were determined to get the most out of its small dimensions. Although she was about half the size of a one-bedroom flat, her working life meant the 'functional aesthetic' that attracted Guylee and David in the first place provided a good basis for the transformation. Their professional space-planning skills allowed them to design an interior that is neat and intelligent, with a kitchen, bathroom and plenty of storage, and can sleep up to six.

The goal was to be as self-sufficient as possible, so solar panels and a composting toilet were installed, along with various heating mechanisms, each tailored to a particular scenario or a specific space. During winter, a wood-burning stove provides the bulk of the on-demand heating, supported by infrared radiant heating within the ceilings of the two main berths. An electric panel radiator ensures that the temperature doesn't drop below a certain level at night. The boat is also heavily insulated for the long northern winters.

'The big challenge was not just finding the time to do all these jobs,' David says, 'but also learning how to do them – everything from installing marine electrics and plumbing to propulsion systems.'

One of the final tasks was to change the colour of the boat to yellow from the original orange. 'When we first looked at it, we thought, this won't take so long,' he adds. 'Couple of months? Maybe six?' It took over a year, and, as with many boats, the work is never quite finished, with the pair constantly thinking of ways to improve it.

By May 2019, all was ready. The couple, with film-maker Jonny Campbell and David's retriever Shackleton on board, set off with no plans to rush the journey. 'It was deliberately slow,' Guylee says of their epic adventure. Indeed, the fact that the boat was built 'for safety, not speed' suited their plans perfectly.

The plan was to reach Tromsø, located in the far north among the Norwegian fjords, before winter set in. Situated at 70° north, the most northerly city in the Arctic would be the couple's base, where they could take stock, settle down a little and look into what they would do next. Guylee and David headed across the channel – navigating the shipping lanes without any problem –

Above
Shackleton, Guylee's trusted retriever, keeps watch.

Opposite
Originally an orange rescue craft based in western Scotland, *Stødig* is now a travelling home – with the accent on the travel.

The Nomadic Lifestyle

Seventy Degrees North

The Nomadic Lifestyle

over to France and then up to Zeebrugge, in Belgium, before heading to Amsterdam, up through IJsselmeer, Holland's biggest lake, and picking up the Kiel Canal towards the Baltic and Copenhagen.

Day-to-day living became focused entirely around the weather, the tides and the landscape. Inevitably, the travellers encountered some bad weather, but for the most part, the boat performed well, and they could appreciate the beauty of their surroundings and the excitement of discovering what lay around the next headland.

Until, that is, while heading up the Kiel Canal, the engine developed serious problems. *Stødig* was towed by the Danish coastguard to just south of Helsingør, and a new starter motor was dispatched from the UK, arriving a week later. Fuelling issues persisted, however, and a rough couple of days tested both the boat and the couple's nerves before they made it, eventually, to Norway. A week spent diagnosing the problem and replacing parts in Varberg, Sweden, uncovered a blockage in the fuel-tank pickup.

But soon *Stødig* was once again a reliable, if rather incongruous, working vessel in northern Europe. Guylee and David grew so used to the calm progress that, as the days and weeks flowed by, the arrival of autumn took them rather by surprise, but they made it to Tromsø in high spirits and on schedule. After a journey marked by detours, excursions and repairs, the appeal of being more settled became evident to both. Guylee, in particular, was happy to rejoin the world of work in their new home, while David headed back to the UK to spend time with his family – a stay that turned out to be longer than expected, owing to lockdown and the global pandemic that would soon engulf the world.

As the compelling short film the couple made of their journey shows so well, there is a friendly, *Yellow Submarine* quality to their beloved boat, especially when seen sailing past towering mountains that, late in the journey, were often flecked with snow. What next for this pair? 'Who knows?' they answer. What is not in doubt is that whatever lies ahead will be slow, novel, tough and enriching. As David says, they hope – like their journey so far – the future will hold adventures 'geared towards finding something we weren't necessarily looking for.'

The challenges of living on a boat

We're fortunate to have a small draft below the waterline, which has allowed us to navigate some very shallow areas and access places that yachts with keels would find difficult. Like any boat, GPS navigation and a depth sounder have been fitted, so that we can safely negotiate any coastline we find ourselves in.

The boat is both small and large, depending on how you look at it. The even profile means that it has a large internal volume for its length. It's never quite large enough, however, and we've had to come up with innovative storage solutions for all of our sailing gear, outdoor and skiing equipment, as well as things for day-to-day living. There are hidden cupboards underneath seats and beds; harder-to-reach areas are used for longterm storage.

Opposite
Guylee on board, taking in some of the stunning scenery he and David have sailed through.

The Nomadic Lifestyle

Above
With an epic journey from the UK to the Norwegian fjords behind them, Guylee and Shackleton take another well-earned swim.

Opposite
The key to the transformation of *Stødig* from a working vessel to a home was the intelligent use of space, as seen in the kitchen.

Seventy Degrees North

Above
The boat's details marry a tough 'functional aesthetic' with a sense of style.

Right
Command and control: a full refit was required to ensure *Stødig* was safe and functional. At a push, she can sleep six.

The Nomadic Lifestyle

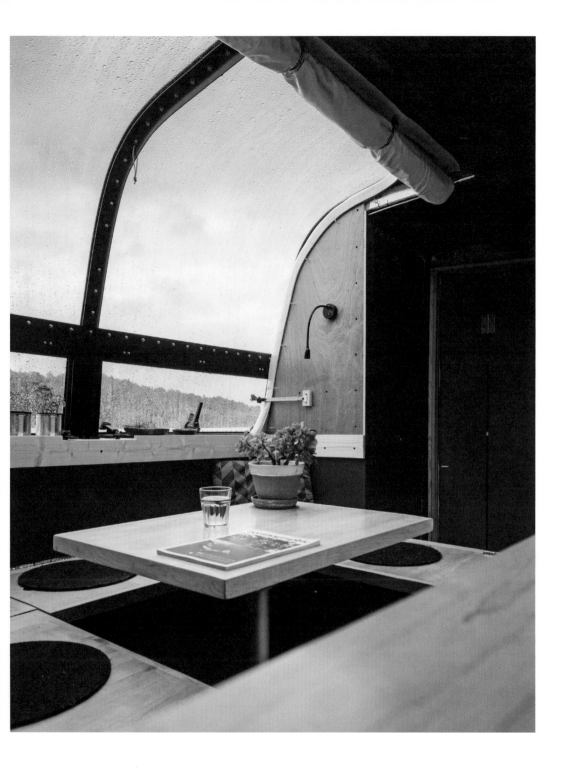

Above
The couple's backgrounds as
architects shines through in
the clever use of space and
well-chosen materials.

Pirates on the Savannah
Soggybottom Shanty, USA

Each boat-dweller's first memory of the seductive magic of water is as different as the homes surrounded by it. For Siva Aiken, it was a childhood spent digging her toes in the sand along the California coast that inspired her life on the river.

Right
The exterior windows were salvaged from an old home being fitted for new; trailer tyres are used as dock bumpers.

Opposite
Siva plays her banjo on the porch of *Soggybottom Shanty*, the pontoon-based boat she built in 2019.

The Nomadic Lifestyle

Pirates on the Savannah

Above
Siva and her Bracco Italianos:
it was the history of America's
inland waterways that attracted
her to the boating lifestyle.

Right
The craft is built from refuse and
recycled materials, a tribute to
the marginalized communities
who once made their home on
the water.

The Nomadic Lifestyle

'The tide pools brought endless joy for me,' Siva remembers, 'with the sea anemones kissing my fingers and tiny crabs wrestling with me from their homes in the cracks of the rock.'

Fast-forward twenty years and these early sensory treats are as vivid as ever, but now recalled aboard her charming boat, *Soggybottom Shanty*, as she travels her 7 m (24 ft)-long vessel along the rivers and lakes of the southern states of South Carolina and Georgia.

The move from the West Coast of her early aquatic memories to the South came about in the summer of 2001. 'I brought my love of water and nature with me,' Siva recalls. The move also meant a change in her relationship with water. She became drawn to – obsessed with, even – the way it navigated the contrasting topographies of these southern regions.

Going mushrooming

As a child, I would often visit my uncle in the Santa Cruz mountains in California. When he discovered that I was too scared to go to the outhouse at night, he began taking me on nighttime hikes to cure my fear of the dark and teach me how to identify trees by their shape and smell.

Once we came across a decomposing tree with a glowing fungus, which started my fascination with mushrooming. One of my favourite dishes is risotto with oyster mushrooms, cooked over an open fire.

By buying local produce and fresh eggs, we meet so many interesting people along the shoreline, who share stories of the shantyboats they have seen in their youth.

Back on the West Coast, days would be spent 'walking the ocean beaches, breathing with the waves, and searching for shells and sea glass treasures.' Today, afternoons are taken up with kayaking along the Savannah River, with its 'mossy overhanging branches and singing cicadas', and see this independent woman at her happiest.

So what turned the head of this musician, artist, writer and dog-lover away from the Pacific to the verdant charms of inland waterways? Bizarrely, perhaps, it was childhood visits to a location as make-believe as they come. 'We vacationed at Disneyland several times,' she says of the original theme park in Anaheim, California, which opened in 1955. But while thousands of youngsters would stand awestruck in front of Goofy and Mickey Mouse, Siva's favourite places in the park all revolved around water, including the Pirates of the Caribbean ride, which is where she saw her first shantyboat. Something clicked.

'There was an automaton man smoking a pipe and rocking in a chair on the front porch of a swamp cabin,' she adds. 'I felt a pull to jump off the ride and move into that little shack, there and then. I would ask my parents to go on that ride endlessly, just to be a part of that scene, even in passing.'

The imagery was the primary driver for her move to the South, leading to further and deeper investigations into the lives of those who lived on the water. 'There is a rich history in America of river people,' Siva says. 'At the turn of the 20th century, the waterways were a dumping ground, and a way to transport logs, coal and merchandise.'

Not surprisingly, rivers in many parts of the US became polluted and were seen as an undesirable place to live. Pushed out to a town's edges, the poor were forced to set up a life along the river. 'They would build huts and flat-bottom shantyboats from the offcuts of lumber that floated down river from mill sites,' she adds. 'Shantyboat villages grew up along the banks, where people could live frugally and away from the ridicule of the town.'

As time passed and restrictions on water pollution grew, the rivers became cleaner and a more desirable place to be. People began to recognize the beauty and desirability of living at the water's edge, and today, many of the area's most expensive and decadent mansions are designed and built along the river. 'This history is one of the reasons I was determined to build my shantyboat from refuse and recycled materials,' Siva says. 'Passing multimillion-dollar

Pirates on the Savannah

homes in my little craft is thumbing my nose at the ridiculous excess in our society – like an art installation reminding people that the beauty of the water is not a commodity for the few, but something to be enjoyed by us all.'

Soggybottom Shanty is a humble vessel, but has considerable presence. When people see it on the water, it brings out their childlike wonder and curiosity, which is just as her owner likes it. 'She has an energy and personality about her,' Siva says, 'a quiet charisma that people fall in love with.'

People love the boat: it speaks of a sense of community, and a history that encompasses America's backwaters and marginalized communities. Whereas other water-borne vessels bristle with technology and invention, *Soggybottom Shanty* is proudly ramshackle. It is this, in Siva's view, which inspires people to dream about recreating a bit of that magic for themselves. Spend a few hours on a boat that is 'reminiscent of a Huck Finn-type craft, pieced together with a touch of fantasy', and you can easily understand why.

The Nomadic Lifestyle

Right
It could be 1922 ... the period
details extend from the fabrics
to the cooking equipment.

Below
Siva in her kitchen, overlooking
the calm waters of the Savannah
River in South Carolina.

Opposite
Soggybottom Shanty, in contrast
to some hi-tech builds, remains
rough and ready.

Pirates on the Savannah

The Maid of Kent
Lady Cat, UK

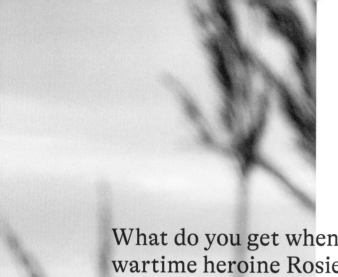

What do you get when you cross the American
wartime heroine Rosie the Riveter with the
Victorian horticulturist Gertrude Jekyll? You get
Jo Pardue, a professional gardener with a lust
for travel, speed and adventure, who can slice holes
through steel while dreaming about the best
place to plant her *Cotinus coggygria*.

Right
The colour scheme of black, red and a tiny dash of yellow are carried through from the exterior. The oil-based eggshell paint on the floor is more flexible than ordinary flooring paint.

Below left
Tucked into the bow, beyond the bathroom, is a cosy cushion-filled room, for a single guest or snuggling up with a good book.

Below right
Jo's bits and bobs have been sourced mostly from French *brocantes* and car-boot sales.

The Nomadic Lifestyle

Learning new skills

My love of France and French design has imprinted itself on *Lady Cat*. The drape at the 'heads' window is made from old linen, dyed black. It was found at a *brocante* in Normandy, as were the vintage red shoe lasts, a zinc stool, some lights and an office chair I reupholstered in a rolled-up piece of antique leather.

Using the power tools waterside on the low deck initially gave me palpitations. But the satisfaction was immense. When putting the porthole in the bathroom, I was balancing on the ledge of the boat and wielding an electric jigsaw, while tentatively cutting out the new hole. It was a small job, but one that gave me the confidence to take on bigger challenges. I sometimes feel that as we get older, we lose faith in ourselves. Working on *Lady Cat* has been the best cure for this – a testament in self-belief.

The 'cosmetic' jobs I have achieved on board so far have been hugely rewarding. *Lady Cat* is now a relaxing bolthole, where I feel inspired, calm and restored.

Having trained in set design, set-building and prop-making for the UK film industry, Jo switched gears to forge a career in still-life photography. That involved learning the arcane arts of reciprocity and darkroom techniques, skills that had fallen into disuse with the advent of the craft-crushing digital revolution. 'It coincided with my daughter's arrival and a deepening reluctance to spend the rest of my life behind a computer screen,' she says.

A major change of direction was no problem for Jo, whose life and career trajectory is nomadic, but seeped in deep research and application. 'I learned very early in life to depend on myself,' she adds. 'People may find me a bit feisty, rambunctious, independent, but I have learned to trust in my intuition. So far, it has guided me away from any serious danger or mess. I crave adventure, and I'm not afraid to go it alone.'

After various reinventions, Jo retrained yet again to study for an RHS Level 2 qualification in horticulture. 'I blew my befuddled menopausal brain with Latin plant names and many exams,' she says, 'but I'm now a very happy and endlessly learning gardener.' Happy enough to settle for what she's achieved? No, and in fact, not even close for such a restless soul. There's a huge garden project and a barn renovation in northern France still in its early stages. And making the most of the freedom offered by her powerful Triumph Bonneville motorbike. And *Lady Cat*.

'I went out on the bike to get some air and think about how long it had been since I really looked at the sky,' Jo remembers. 'What I needed, I decided, was a boat. It was meant to be a many-layered solution: a place to escape the city smoke, a new project to do up and repair, somewhere to play, go wild swimming, a bolthole, a room of one's own, potential canalside accommodation for my daughter at some point in the future, somewhere to paint clouds, draw, do yoga.'

Eventually, her musings led her to a historic Dutch barge at Roydon, Essex, on what she describes as 'a stinky canalside mooring', where it stood alone, apart from a few narrowboats. *Vrouwe Catharina* was the third vessel I looked at,' she says, 'and I knew I wanted to rescue and revive her. She was covered in leaves and detritus and a little sad, but with a lot of potential that I believed I could manage. I felt immediately drawn to her.'

The boat that would soon become *Lady Cat* had, Jo notes, a 'sense of strength and beauty' about her. 'Even though her lee boards and mast were long gone,' she adds, 'I felt a huge tenderness towards this inanimate thing. I was aware that a seaworthy vessel would be a step too far for me at this point. I did, however, have every confidence that I had the necessary skills to bring *Lady Cat* back to life. I'm a practical girl, raised on a farm, and I

The Maid of Kent

like being able to make good. I'm not at all shy of effusing about my ever-expanding tool collection, and I'm not afraid of an angle grinder or a pipe bender.'

Jo needed a professional skipper to navigate her iron lady from the Hertfordshire/Essex borders to its new home on the Medway in Kent, a two-day voyage via a complex web of rivers, canals, the Thames Barrier and seemingly endless locks – a journey that grew more urgent as the autumn of 2020 wore on, as many of the locks close in October for winter. Enter marine surveyor Stefan Fritz, who turned up, Jo says, 'in the dark, with fuel, tools, good humour and an exceeding amount of patience. I knew we were in safe hands.'

Other good omens were to come. As *Lady Cat* motored along a canal outside London, a woman in rain-soaked pyjamas, dressing gown and slippers chased Jo along the towpath, asking if this was 'Anna's boat'. Jo told her it was, or had been. 'The lady promised me I'd never forget my first voyage, and she was right,' Jo says.

'*Lady Cat* and I will continue our journey ahead after a few more repairs, some licks of paint and a lot of joy,' Jo adds. 'She is a beautiful lady who embraces me each time I arrive, sometimes weighed down with the burdens of life. She gives me time to daydream and appreciate a good spanner collection. I might look for a non-tidal Thames spot next, where I can swim and be more readily able to take wee sojourns without fear of navigational misdemeanours. Our wonderful journey has just begun. Would I do it all again? I surely would. And I have a welding course booked in.'

The Nomadic Lifestyle

Above
The desk, covered in zinc sheeting, is supported at one end by a wall mount and an adjustable trestle at the other.

Right
The bed sits atop the 'engine room', a six-cylinder Mercedes unit, and slides to the side when the engine needs to run.

Opposite
A practical kitchen, with plenty of storage and zinc splashbacks. Recycled offcuts from the desk provide ample cooking space.

Overleaf
The living area is warmed by the wood-burner, inherited from the previous owner, which just needed a little heat-resistant paint to spruce it up.

The Maid of Kent

The Nomadic Lifestyle

The Maid of Kent

Space to Roam
Raumschiff, Germany

Raumschiff is made from aluminium, which is durable, lightweight and requires less maintenance than its fibreglass counterparts.

When you were a child, did you dream of piloting a spacecraft through a galaxy far, far away? For Thea and Moritz, such dreams have become a slightly more earthbound reality, thanks to their very own *Raumschiff* (German for 'spaceship'), whose modest dimensions were designed for meandering as the mood takes them along Europe's vast network of waterways.

Thea, a communications designer and strategist, is convinced that small spaces are only good when they are liveable. Moritz is a product designer, boat-builder and master at recycling, who never ceases to prove that old, worn-out things can be turned into something completely new if properly rebuilt. *Raumschiff* was born from their mutual desire to live sustainably on the water, an environment that has always felt like home.

The joys and challenges of living on a boat

In winter, we stay on-grid, because the solar gain isn't enough to supply us with electricity. We rent a berth so that we have access to services. The idea of a home port is common in Germany.

Going wherever you want with your own house is an incredibly liberating feeling – we've even sailed the boat to parties a few times. Living on board is also about discovering new things. The natural world is much closer – one time we saw a grey heron surfing on a magpie. Most evenings, we just sit and gaze at the water and the stars while listening to the nightingales sing.

In summer, we produce our own electricity with the help of a photovoltaic system. It's wonderful to eat food made using solar energy, and run our dinghy on it. If the sun hasn't shone for long enough, however, then it's cold showers in the morning.

'Even before we had a boat, we often found ourselves by rivers or lakes to recharge our batteries,' says Thea. 'Maybe it was the silvery, shiny surface, or the reflection of the sky, or maybe it cannot be explained rationally. We both feel that proximity to water means proximity to nature – being exposed to weather, winds, waves, the sun, and seeing animals, landscapes and natural phenomena, which we would never see tucked in between four concrete walls on land.'

The project took six months of planning, a 650 km (400 mile)-long trip to their berth in Berlin after collecting *Raumschiff* from Duisburg, and eighteen months of self-building before they could move in. It would have been even longer and cost far more had they not decided to use the hull of an existing speedboat as a pre-prepared base. 'She is made entirely from aluminium, so we didn't need to sand her down, treat rust or repaint,' Moritz explains. 'We would never have been able to build her ourselves – she is one of the first aluminium boats to be welded entirely by robots, ensuring insane build precision.'

The aim from the start was to create a small, self-sufficient space to minimize energy costs and enable off-grid living in the summer, thanks to a photovoltaic system. 'It's a fantastic feeling to eat a solar cake,' laughs Thea. Add in plentiful insulation, heating from a highly efficient pellet stove, a separating toilet and multiple water-filtration systems, and *Raumschiff* is ready to chart a course for anywhere the couple wish to go, with no more effort than firing up the engine.

There are caveats, however. 'The boat travels much more slowly than you might think,' Moritz admits. 'She's rated for 900 hp, and used to have three very large outboards on the stern, which we replaced with a 60 hp outboard. We're planning a new stern to reduce water resistance and enable us to go a little faster.'

In the winter, travel is restricted somewhat by the fact that they have to remain on-grid, so the couple pays monthly rent for a berth in the harbour in Potsdam, near Berlin, where they have access to electricity and water.

Looking to the future

With many boaters in Germany over sixty, our water-borne communities need more young people. There are fewer such communities here than in the Netherlands or the UK. Through Instagram we have made contact with lots of people who live on boats, but they are scattered across the country. At the moment, we're planning a journey towards France – four people and two boats. We are looking forward to meeting fellow boat-dwellers on our travels.

So are they really true nomads at heart? 'It sounds cheesy, but going wherever you want with your own house is an incredibly beautiful and liberating feeling,' Thea says. 'Since we've

The Nomadic Lifestyle

been living on the boat, even the everyday feels like being on holiday. The places we stay can be so incredibly beautiful – sometimes we just cast off in the evening, go out, then anchor and sleep out on the lake. In the morning, we'll jump into the water naked while still drowsy, before driving back and going to work.'

She adds: 'But we have come to realize that lingering to stop and enjoy the beauty around us is just as important as moving on. We look for the possibilities in the moment, and that's how we view travelling. When the sun is right, we sit down in our paddleboat and eat tacos while watching the sun set. When we get the opportunity to travel, we just do it.'

Thea captains *Raumschiff* over the calm waters of the Havel River, while Moritz takes in the stunning scenery.

Space to Roam

Left
Much on the ship is recycled, including the sink, which is made from an old drain pipe. A tinted window makes the white-painted shower appear yellow or purple.

Below
Photos show how *Raumschiff* looked when it was purchased, a reminder of how much planning went into the build.

The Nomadic Lifestyle

Right
In the living room, the sofa is made from a recycled trampoline and can sleep two. The cushions and upholstery can be taken up to the roof.

Below
The kitchen-unit doors are also handmade, coated with high-quality linoleum. A space-saving espresso machine and a three-way tap complete the look.

Space to Roam

Moritz and Thea on the roof; below them is a self-portrait by Anna Albert, painted onto the door. The artist sees her work as a way to connect people, and hopes that Thea and Moritz will continue to meet artists who will repaint the door, so that it becomes a stunning graffiti wall.

The Nomadic Lifestyle

Above
The rug was purchased in Morocco and holds fond memories, as does the silver sign, which bears the name of the couple's former boat.

Right
The hallway is lined with old printing plates; in the evening, the lights of the city and reflections on the water give the feeling of being afloat in space.

Space to Roam

The Nomadic Lifestyle

Below
A simple wooden rowing boat
transports the couple to shore
when the boat is not moored up.

Opposite
On top of their spacecraft:
it is easy to see where the
inspiration for *Raumschiff*'s
name came from.

Space to Roam

Renovating

Decorating &

Living on the water isn't always easy. Yet for some, the chance to restore or transform a boat is part of the magic. In exchange for months, or often years, of hard graft, the rewards can be stunning: unique and deeply personal vessels that speak to their owners' abilities to turn dreams into reality.

Renovating & Decorating

At the Wheel: *Oldenburg,* Denmark

The phrase 'if walls could talk' is normally reserved for houses, yet in the case of *Oldenburg*, a river barge that dates from 1908, it could apply just as well to boats. Having spent most of its life as a working craft, it was bought by Greenpeace in 1993 as a floating gallery. Seven years later, it graduated to the third phase of its long life: as the home of Lis and Ove, and a holiday home for their family and wide circle of friends.

Renovating & Decorating

At the Wheel

But the transformation was far from easy – or cheap. Lis and Ove could immediately see the possibilities, but some warned them off the whole enterprise. 'They simply could not see the huge potential that we did,' Ove says. 'It was not an elderly-friendly choice, in other words, which is how they put it.'

Foraging for food

Lis is very creative and always up for new adventures. She learned an old knitting technique, and ended up demonstrating it at the local museum in Køge. Wherever she goes, she forages for food, sometimes right by her feet: asparagus, beach cabbage, wild garlic, wild onions, sea sandwort, all of which are easy to find if you know where to look.

We are always searching for new ways to eat seafood, and all kinds of fish. Porbeagle (mackerel shark) is one of them – wonderful. Each year, we gather oysters with friends, just north of Jutland. We are outside more now than when we lived on land, and all that extra light helps to maintain a bright mind and positive attitude all year round.

The expressions of concern were voiced at a time when the couple were in their late fifties (they are now in their seventies). 'But we had so many ideas and plans for the boat that we didn't care about how much work needed to be done,' Ove continues. The biggest draw for the couple was the boat's enormous size, which allowed them to create a spacious home that could accommodate the whole family. 'That was very important for us,' Lis adds.

From the wheelhouse down, significant work was needed. The cramped space where a crew of two or three would be accommodated was simply too small for their ambitious plans. One of the first jobs was to expand it to create what is now a stunning dining area with a long table; it is a wonderful point of entry onto *Oldenburg*.

Other work included the installation of underfloor heating and solar cells on the roof. There is also a spacious living room, a good-sized kitchen, a bathroom, two bedrooms and a walk-in closet. Outside is a terrace at the stern and a sun deck. Throughout, the couple's keen eye for colour and the use of a few high-quality pieces have resulted in a cool interior with contrasting textures and an elegant colour palette. Their shared ambition had always been to build something that would be both beautiful and functional, without compromising on style and comfort.

Ironically, it was Lis and Ove's reluctance to embark on extensive repairs to their rented property in Denmark that led to their new life on *Oldenburg*. 'We knew we didn't want to spend time and energy on another renovation,' Ove says. 'We were ready for a fresh start and a new adventure. We put the house up for sale, and within eight days it sold for the highest price achieved in the area, so the timing was good. Lis thought that we could live more cheaply, retire earlier and have a life with less stress if we bought a houseboat instead of a house, so that's what we did. We haven't missed anything by moving from land to water.'

Downsizing and organizing

The biggest issue when we moved onto the boat was making room for our possessions. We ended up selling a lot of furniture and things we didn't need, and kept only those items that had a practical or a personal significance.

We have a workshop on the dock where we store things we don't need on board, like outdoor furniture and cushions, as well as a bench in the wheelhouse for holiday decorations and crafting supplies, underbed storage and a walk-in closet behind the living room. It's about reducing your possessions to fit your life.

Life aboard is nothing new for this industrious pair. 'Our sailing adventures go back a long way,' says Lis, a self-employed hairdresser who grew up in Copenhagen and spent childhood summers on the coast. 'We had a wooden fishing cutter, and would catch herring, plaice, sea trout and large cod in nets. It felt like pulling diamonds from the water.'

Ove, now seventy-four, is also from Copenhagen and started out as a salesman in a computer company, before becoming director of marketing at Denmark's largest phone company. His own summers as a child were spent at the family's holiday home, in the next village

Renovating & Decorating

Right
Ove positions fenders to
prevent damage to the boat
while it is moored up.

Below
The fully working wheelhouse
was too small, so it was
expanded to make room for
a spacious dining area.

At the Wheel

Renovating & Decorating

along from where Lis and her family had their vacations. The irony of holidays spent just a few miles apart is not lost on the pair.

Living on the water has created many wonderful memories for the couple. 'Too many to list,' they say. 'All of our Christmas dinners in the wheelhouse with our children and grandchildren have been memorable. *Oldenburg* is always dressed for Christmas.'

But the real highlight for the couple was the wedding of their daughter Christina, which took place on deck with 100 guests standing on the quay, watching the ceremony. 'Afterwards there was a party in a workshop on the quayside,' recalls Lis. '*Oldenburg*, the scene of so many wonderful family moments over the years, was firmly in view to all, a welcome and beloved guest at the wedding.'

This dramatic boat, with over 100 years on the water, has become a member of the family, which, one suspects, will be enjoyed and treasured by the next generation as much as she has been by the determined and enterprising Lis and Ove for the past twenty years.

Above
Below deck, natural light floods through portholes and skylights to the living area. Wooden furniture and a comfy sofa create an inviting and relaxed space.

Opposite
The rear of the wheelhouse now houses a long table with enough room to seat all the family.

At the Wheel

Left
Every aspect of the design has been thoughtfully considered, including the extra storage built beneath the stairs.

Below
A three-quarter length wall with a large window partitions the kitchen to form the living space.

Opposite
One of the two bedrooms, with sleek, panelled walls that are a nod to traditional boat interiors.

Renovating & Decorating

At the Wheel

Above
Planning is an essential part
of boat travel, to ensure it
is a pleasurable experience
and to facilitate help in case
of emergencies.

Left
Making good use of the breeze
that rolls across the water, Lis
hangs out the family washing.

Opposite
The warm colour scheme
continues into the bathroom,
with a full-sized bath for
relaxing in at the end of a
hard day's sailing.

Renovating & Decorating

At the Wheel

Water Babies
Graaf Floris V, Netherlands

Above and opposite
Annelies's Scandinavian-inspired home backs onto a large garden. Inside, a play area gives her children the space to get creative.

Overleaf
A decked area provides not only the perfect jumping-off point, but also somewhere to relax in the evenings and enjoy the changing seasons.

The idea of living afloat is a giant plunge into the unknown for those who can't imagine a home that isn't planted on solid ground with enough space to store a lifetime of possessions – even if most of them are long-forgotten dust traps. Annelies Dorsman's story is the opposite of that. A true water baby who has spent nearly all of her thirty-seven years living on the canals of Amsterdam, she can't imagine any other kind of existence.

Renovating & Decorating

Water Babies

Renovating & Decorating

Water Babies

Every day I wake up and say 'thank you' for being able to live here. The scale of the windows really brings the outside in, allowing us to live with nature, immersed in the seasons.

Through our windows we can see a wonderful view of the canal. Every morning, the water is different: the dew, the first thin layers of ice, the little ducks in spring, and the gorgeous display of yellows and reds in autumn.

The boat is a special place for so many reasons. The children having such wonderful access to nature right on their doorstep is something you can't put a price on. We consider ourselves very fortunate, indeed.

'In the 1960s, when my parents were starting a family, it was hard to find a home in the city,' Annelies says. 'Land is very limited, so houses were expensive and living on the water was much cheaper. My parents bought a traditional inland boat to live on, but after three years they discovered severe leakages that couldn't be repaired. So they bought a concrete tank and my father and grandfather built a new houseboat on top of it. My older sisters were born on the original boat, and my brother and I were born on the houseboat, where I lived until I got married. My mother still lives on it.'

Marriage took Annelies ashore for eighteen months when she and her husband Hans moved into a bricks-and-mortar house in the suburb of Amsterdam-Zuidoost. But that, she says, was just part of a grander scheme. 'We wanted to design our own home and began looking for building plots. Then a place on the dyke where I grew up came up for sale, and we realized it was perfect for us. There was an old boat there, which we sold to make room for our houseboat.'

Once the couple had their new house, it was time to turn it into a home. 'We styled the boat from scratch, and wanted as big a space as possible downstairs,' Annelies adds. 'We loved the big windows of our first home, the dark anthracite frames and the view, and have incorporated those elements into the design. Our interior changes every year: a new wallpaper is added, or cushions are replaced. I think of my style as Scandinavian with a warm touch – starting with a soft base, and then adding colour. Our home has evolved organically over the years, but there are always soft pinks and mint green. Last year, shades of lilac crept in. We like making these changes.'

Opposite
Annelies favours a minimalist approach to interior design, using a blend of textures and soft hues to make her sleek and modern home feel warm and inviting.

Renovating & Decorating

Water Babies

Renovating & Decorating

Something else that changed the lives of Annelies and Hans was the arrival of their children, Scott and Skye. Like their mum, most of their lives have so far been spent on the water. 'Growing up on a houseboat feels normal,' Annelies says. 'It is unusual, but we have a big garden and a view of the water. There is so much to see and to do. We made a play area behind the sofa, and there is a bench with drawers and colourful crates, so it's easy to sort the toys. Of course, the children need their own space, but I love it in the evenings when the toys are all put away. It's easier to relax when the kids are asleep.'

The houseboat, *Graaf Floris V*, is named partly for the 13th-century nobleman who first granted Amsterdam its prized water rights, and partly for the two dogs Annelies had as a child. In another link to her childhood, her home is moored close to the wharf where she grew up – a once-bustling boat-builder's yard that became a haven for squatters and budding young artists and craftspeople after falling into disrepair in the 1980s. Today, the area has been redeveloped and a new generation of creatives and entrepreneurs have transformed it into a fashionable quarter, echoing those early years.

'The area has changed massively,' Annelies says. 'My parents were among the first to settle here, when it was mostly fields and the residential areas next to the dyke didn't exist. Now, many people can't afford to live here. But I love the neighbourhood: my father and grandfather worked on the wharf, and there are lots of new, cool restaurants popping up in the old hangars where they would build the boats. When we go out for dinner, with or without the children, we tend to go there.'

She pauses to consider her water-based existence. 'Never say never, but it would have to be something very special to persuade us to move from this place. It's completely different to other parts of the city. It feels more free – more raw.'

So speaks a true veteran of life on the water.

Historic beginnings

The popularity of houseboats in Amsterdam is in step with a rediscovery of the pleasure of being on the water. Houseboats were formerly seen as a cheap alternative to land-based homes, and the waterways were largely forgotten.

In the 1960s, more and more houseboats – complete with running water and electricity – began to appear as a solution to the demand for more housing. Known as *woonarks*, they sat alongside the original boats and barges, some of which dated back a century or more – a legacy of the city's seafaring and maritime trading days.

The Dutch government capped the number of houseboat permits to 2,400 to prevent overcrowding on the canals, thus creating a limited-edition way of living. Today, floating homes command the same prices as those made from bricks and mortar.

Opposite
Being together as a family is important to Annelies and Hans. When not strolling around the city, they spend most of their time at home.

Water Babies

Above
Annelies's design embraces the principles of *lagom* – taking the time to find the right piece for the right space – as seen in the cosy seating area in the garden.

Opposite left
One of Annelies's design rules is to ensure that each space has the same vibe by using the same colours and materials.

Opposite right
The Scandinavian-inspired design creates a soothing atmosphere and is perfect for a child's bedroom.

Water Babies

Renovating & Decorating

Above
The considered use of light and wooden furniture creates a warm and inviting dining area; the display of dried grasses adds a natural and relaxed layer.

Right
A small office off the dining room is the perfect place to work, with a view of water and wildlife.

Opposite
The kitchen was the only room that was fully designed when they moved in; the rest of the interior evolved organically.

Water Babies

Family Home
This One Floats, UK

Opposite
On deck, Christina and Aluki take in the views; the walk-on skylight allows natural light to flood into the living area below.

Most young couples with a baby on the way would baulk at the idea of moving house, never mind renovating a 1960s Dutch barge from bare-hull condition into a contemporary three-bedroom family home. Yet that's exactly what Christina Miles and her partner Rohan Tully did in eighteen months. So successful was the result that they have since established their own business, Isla Yachts, to help others bring their living-afloat dreams to life.

Family Home

'It can be daunting, so we wanted to make it possible for people to take that leap of faith,' Christina explains. Not that they were absolute beginners at the restoration game, or indeed boats: Rohan, an established property developer who is currently managing a development of twelve flats, grew up around them and has plenty of experience with both boats and refurbishments.

'There is no way we could have done this without his expertise,' she adds. 'There's a huge difference between building boats and building houses. With boats, you have to accommodate the moving tide, expanding and retracting steel.'

Of course, the upside is not having to deal with the building and planning restrictions that come with bricks and mortar, so there is plenty of scope to get creative. And this turned out to be one heck of a creative project, not least thanks to Christina's flair for interior design, replete with bold colours and patterns that are a sophisticated change from the usual 'homely' barge style.

Moorings and the community

We prefer being further upriver as there is less traffic. No passenger ferries means no wash constantly rocking our boat. West London has always been home for us, and there is more wildlife upstream, which always adds colour to the day.

Once in the mooring, we were welcomed into an incredible community that supports each other in every way. There is a broad mix of ages, households and professions, with everyone united in their efforts to support one another – much needed in a way of life that requires daily problem-solving.

Moorings are few and far between in London, especially for a boat 30 m (98 ft) in length. We had already cut it down from 40 m (over 130 ft), and were very lucky to find this mooring as it was being built.

But first, the backstory: desperate to move out of their cramped flat in central London, but not wanting to drift too far from friends, family and work, Christina and Rohan had spent a couple of years looking for the right vessel to convert. With the clock ticking down to the birth of daughter Elara, now two, they discovered a hulking 1965 Belgian Spitz, a former container ship that had once plied Europe's

Renovating & Decorating

waterways and is now home to their small family, including an Alaskan Klee Kai – a smaller version of the Siberian husky – named Aluki.

Starting your own project

A blank canvas is the best way to embark on a project. The exterior of our boat was a good starting point, but it was the vast internal space that really got us thinking about the possibilities.

We look for space that can be easily adapted, at how it sits in the water and how windows might be positioned to maximize the views. Each boat is different, but as with every home renovation project, it's what you can do with the space that counts.

Living by the water has always been something we wanted to do, so deciding to live on a boat was an easy choice, especially when compared to the cost of waterside living on land.

'We'd driven out to Ghent to see it,' remembers Christina. 'As we opened up some of the steel on the roof, it was so exciting to see the big, dark space become flooded with light. It was a blank canvas, and a big one – we could build whatever crazy designs we wanted, with no building restrictions.'

Purchase completed, Rohan spent ten days sailing the barge from Ghent to a shipyard in Harlingen for some radical surgery. 'Finding a sizeable mooring in London was a killer,' he muses, ruefully. 'So much so that it was easier and cheaper to buy a boat, snip a chunk out the middle and stick it back together. Luckily, that's no biggie for the Dutch shipyards.'

A couple of months later, in the depths of winter, Rohan, his dad and a few friends finally brought the barge home across the Channel, delayed only slightly by being arrested early in the voyage. Luckily, after a 'brief discussion' and production of the appropriate paperwork, they were allowed to continue their journey in what was then little more than a tank.

'No running water, no heating, half a loo and half of Belgium's beer supply,' laughs Christina. 'I cannot describe the smell when I

Family Home

Left
A blank canvas to begin with, the bathroom now boasts beautiful tiles and practical twin sinks.

Opposite
The boat's scale means there is plenty of room for entertaining on the open deck.

Previous pages
Elara uses one of the portholes as an impromptu drawing board.

Renovating & Decorating

met them on the other side, as they moored at slack tide on the River Medway.'

An intensive period of renovation ensued, including a painful twenty-four-hour wait to see if the new cement ballast – vital for keeping the boat stable and lower in the water – had set evenly. (Reader, it had.) A series of setbacks, coupled with frustration over temporary living arrangements, led the family to move in before the electrics and plumbing were resolved.

'We made do with extension cables and portable heaters for a while,' she says. 'We were happy to do that for the thrill of waking up that first morning and looking out the window.'

Ah yes, the windows – super-sized portholes looking directly over the water at their island mooring in the Thames, creating the impression of actually being *in* the river.

'The views we get of the wildlife blow us away,' Christina adds. 'We once had nine swans outside our window, and on many occasions have sat out on deck watching seals swim by. The colours of the water at sunrise or through the fog on a cold day are just stunning. To go back to living on land again … ,' she pauses. 'It would have to be something pretty special. I'm not sure if we could ever live next to a road again.'

Family Home

Above
The dining area also makes the most of super-sized portholes and Christina's keen eye for design detail.

Right
Initially, Christina wanted a fireplace in the living room, but, she says, 'that would mean a chimney coming out of the deck, and then Rohan would have to see if he could make it possible.'

Opposite
The couple's daughter has grown up knowing only *This One Floats* as her home.

Overleaf
The kitchen has become a favourite spot for the family. 'We didn't expect this room to be such a feature, and it really is,' Christina says.

Renovating & Decorating

Family Home

Renovating & Decorating

Family Home

Cargo Barge Reinvention
Bosco, UK

Transforming the vast carcass of a Dutch barge from grain and coal transporter into a spectacular modern family home, complete with a Glacier Mint-style winter garden on deck and a banquette-lined cinema room smuggled into the bow, is no small undertaking. But with one similar conversion already under their belts, Claire Bunten and Alistair Langhorne couldn't resist *Bosco*'s potential.

Having designed a number of other boats already, we know what works and what doesn't for life on the water. Areas to focus on are finding the balance between inside and outside space, capturing views while maintaining privacy, designing sightlines from the wheelhouse so the boat can still be navigable, and locating services so that they work effectively both on a mooring and at sea.

Insulation is key to creating a comfortable environment. The type of insulation we used ensures there's no build up of cold or moisture, reducing heat loss in the winter. We were also conscious of our impact on the environment, so we used reclaimed materials wherever possible, including the stone floor in the bathroom, salvaged from a designer boutique in Sloane Avenue, and the floor in the garden room, made from sanded-down scaffolding boards.

Luxuries include a cinema room tucked into the bow of the boat, along with the indoor/outdoor space created by opening up the winter garden's four doors in summer.

Opposite
Inside is a calm, well-ordered space, a legacy of the original hold being divided into three sections at the build stage. Above the 'Tulip' table is a pendant light designed by Seppo Koho.

Over a decade earlier, they had turned their first Dutch barge, *L'Alliance*, into a studio office for their growing business (LAB Architects), so when *Bosco* hove into view, they knew what they were letting themselves in for – although, Claire admits, 'it's a bit like having a second baby; you forget the hard work it took to create the first one.'

And was this houseboat baby, how shall we say, planned? Not exactly. 'Sikander, a guy in Bordeaux who had sold us the first barge, got in touch and said he would give us a really good price for this one. At 5 × 38 m (16 × 125 ft), the empty hold was seductive, and he had already put in fourteen brass portholes, which suggested the rhythm for the rooms. And so it came to pass that we – slightly accidentally – bought a second boat.'

What began as a commercially driven project quickly morphed into a delightful opportunity to trade conventional living in a four-bedroom Fulham townhouse for an altogether more relaxed lifestyle across the river in Lombard Wharf, Battersea, where the couple owned a mooring at Oyster Pier with a rare 120-year lease. 'We had outgrown where we lived before,' she adds. 'Our children were now teenagers, and having been around boats since they were tiny, they were keen to have a river-living adventure. So we decided to make the move.'

The renovation took nine months and involved a complete refit and re-engineering to convert an erstwhile working barge into 211 m^2 (2,270 sq ft) of comfortable family home. To save time and money, the work was carried out while *Bosco* was moored upriver at Isleworth. 'She arrived in twenty-six sections,' explains Alistair. 'Our contractors from Lowestoft welded everything together.'

Using the position of the portholes as design parameters, the couple carved up the hold into three sections – the master suite in the stern, children's bedrooms in the bow, and family spaces in between, including the open-plan dining area and kitchen. Heating is provided by a wood-burning stove and cast-iron radiators, and the entire structure has 'fridge-like insulation' to prevent cold spots and humidity.

'We also had to tackle some not insignificant technical challenges,' Alistair adds, 'including the requirement to co-locate most of the bathroom and washing services in one place, so that the boat can be connected with shore facilities for power and waste disposal. And we kept the wheelhouse, so we can still move her if we want to.'

For Claire, there was one non-negotiable design element: room for some kind of garden had to be made on board. From this germ of an idea grew a striking glass box on a mirrored plinth, inspired by the proportions of an industrial shipping container and filled with temperate plants, a vine and lemon trees.

Cargo Barge Reinvention

Renovating & Decorating

The boat provides our family with a unique way of living. It's a privilege we never take for granted.

We live in the centre of a busy city, surrounded by highrise living, and can honestly say we are so blessed to be able to swim with seals, get the paddleboards out when friends come over, even collect the children from parties in our dinghy. The dinghy is also our main means of transport to the office, bypassing the busy public-transport network.

We have so many wonderful memories, of what we have achieved and experienced, and look forward to many more.

Above
Clean lines are key to a visually calm interior, an aesthetic at which Claire and Alistair excel.

Opposite
The couple's previous experience with fitting out boats shines through in the intelligent use of space. The marble countertop extends into an island with room to work or have breakfast.

Overleaf
The garden room, inspired by a (transparent) shipping container resting on mirrored plinths, is filled with greenery and is a wonderfully peaceful environment.

In warm weather, all four doors can be opened to create an inside/outside experience, while light floods in – even on the coldest days – through the heavy glazing.

Memorable moments bob through barge life like ducks on the river. 'The water constantly bouncing light around the space, having sundowners on deck and the only noise coming from the resident moorhen, it's all such an antidote to London life,' Claire enthuses. 'Oyster Pier is a real community. The kids love inviting their friends over, as it's such a different environment. Of course, there are the odd technical hitches that you have to expect when living on a boat, like the occasional power cut. Accessing the pier can also be a bit challenging in winter. You need to make a commitment to boat life and learn how to live it – it's not like living in a serviced apartment. But then the feeling of being gently rocked to sleep makes up for all that.'

Renovating & Decorating

Cargo Barge Reinvention

Above
An open stairway, with a
log-burner tucked beneath,
leads down from the garden
room to the lower level; oak
parquet flooring is used
throughout.

Opposite
The bedroom typifies Claire and
Alistair's approach: a feeling of
calm and luxury in a robust and
hardworking setting. The
four-poster bed was too large for
the room, so the couple simply
cut it down to size.

172   Renovating & Decorating

Cargo Barge Reinvention

Renovating & Decorating

Right
Floating on a floating craft: the
occasional 1970s touch, as seen
in this Eero Aarnio chair design,
makes *Bosco* a cool home.

Opposite
The children's bedrooms were
the perfect place to introduce
pops of colour; they were
designed for socializing and
study, as well as sleeping.

Cargo Barge Reinvention

Award-winning artists on a Dutch sailing clipper; photographers on a lightship off the Thames Estuary; a former model based on a houseboat in Holland: combining living and working on the water calls for creativity, focus and flair, and these work-from-home vessels show what can be achieved.

Creative

Channels

Creative Channels

For someone who has yet to reach thirty, Jeanne de Kroon has squeezed in more than the average number of lives. Her teen years took her from her family home in Amsterdam to New York, where her stunning looks could have guaranteed a successful modelling career. But after a few months in front of the camera, she was already doubting her choice.

Above
Boots for walking: bags for shopping – 'the textiles make the boat what it is'.

Opposite
Colour everywhere: Jeanne's interior-design taste reflects her extensive travels across the world and the inspirational women she's met along the way.

Life in Full Colour
Zazi Houseboat, Netherlands

Left
One-time model Jeanne with one of the two rescue hens with whom she shares her home and small garden.

Below
Having grown up with stories of her grandfather and his life on boats, Jeanne knew the moment she found a houseboat for rent that it would be her home.

Opposite
'As a traveller,' Jeanne says, 'a houseboat really feels like the best home I can imagine in the Netherlands.'

Overleaf
Having spent years living out of a suitcase, Jeanne's dresses now hang all over the houseboat. Each item in her home is a celebration of artisanal craft and the weaving of the women's narratives in fabric.

Creative Channels

Life in Full Colour

Creative Channels

Life in Full Colour

Instead, Jeanne accepted a friend's invitation to sample life in the more bohemian quarters of Berlin and study philosophy, only to be disappointed by the near-total absence of women's achievements in the narrative. Before long, she decided that she needed broader, first-hand experiences to provide meaning to her life, so she dropped out and began building up the small vintage-clothing business she had started to help pay her way.

Then the journey that had taken her from Amsterdam to New York and Berlin took another turn in India, and eventually led to the Amazon rainforest. 'I went in search of something more than what Western philosophy had to offer,' she explains. 'I wanted to understand pagan traditions, herbalism and clothing that could be traced back to a place and time. We had all this in Europe once.'

How have you made your home your own?

Colours are your best friend. A light home works so beautifully in a sun-drenched country, but when you live on a boat in the Amsterdam canals, colour is important to warm up the space. Small rooms are better in darker, warmer colours, and you can never have too much colour. My advice is to just go for it!

We decide for ourselves what 'art' looks like. I don't really own any art, although I come from a family of artists. My home is full of things that I have turned into art by giving them a special role, from small items found in nature, like a dried flower from Ethiopia to the pieces of fabric hanging everywhere. Everyone has special objects that make a home.

Over the past ten years, Jeanne has visited some of the most beautiful, remote and dangerous places in the world, from the mountains of Afghanistan and Kurdistan to the rivers and rainforests of South America, Morocco to the heart of Africa. The quest continues, and wherever she ventures, she seeks out craftswomen whose creations she sells through her company, Zazi Vintage.

Finally, Jeanne has found a way to blend her wanderlust with her passion for promoting the interests of women. But while her travels are by no means at an end, she has returned to her roots in Amsterdam – if canals can be said to have roots, that is. Soon after her return, she found an ageing houseboat for rent on one of the city's northern canals. 'For travellers,' she says, 'a houseboat is the ultimate way to feel like you're on holiday at home.'

Dating back to the 1970s, the all-wooden craft was a little dowdy for her tastes, so she painted it raspberry-pink. The interior is a tumult of colours, not only as the result of the extraordinarily vivid textiles carried back from her travels, but also from her own clothes, which hang in every available nook and cranny.

'I always have my dresses hanging all over the place,' she explains. 'I'm a girl living alone on a pink houseboat, so why not? The textiles make my home what it is: a colourful bubble of memories. I love my old boat, even though something is always going wrong – the heating fails, or I tie it up in a panic when the wind starts to blow. But every morning I wake up and think, this is so cool! I grew up in cities where you never really get to know your neighbours, but boat life brings the community together – we say hello, exchange gifts, and even have a swim club. My bedroom opens up straight onto the canal, and as it's one of the cleaner waterways, I can wake up and jump right in.'

Living afloat also brings unexpected spiritual benefits. 'My father makes documentaries on the magic of light in paintings,' Jeanne adds. 'We would go to the beach and he would tell me to not just look, but also to watch and observe. It's the Buddhist way of finding the transcendental in the ordinary. From early morning cold dips to hanging my laundry alongside a family of swans, hearing the raindrops on the roof to observing the ever-changing light, life on the water is pretty perfect for that.'

There are other, more homely – if unusual – delights to be found. Jeanne points out two chickens who are scrabbling about on the deck.

Creative Channels

Some boat-owners embrace the minimal, but not here: a riot of colour fills the houseboat, which cheers Jeanne up on those grey, northern European days.

'I have two rescue hens who live with me and follow me everywhere I go. I've had many parties in the little garden with the chickens on the table eating with us. A houseboat really feels like the best home I can imagine in a place like the Netherlands.'

Finding inspiration everywhere

Whenever I visit communities around the world, I always feel inspired when I come home, and will often embark on more research as a result. All over Europe there is the imprint of history, perhaps in the form of a piece of clothing, which can be traced back to a place and time.

This idea has helped me transform my home into what it is – in many ways, a collection of love letters from women I have met on my travels. The most incredible stories emerge through fabric. It's like the Buddhist way of explaining the world, and looking beyond what you see in front of you.

Further inspiration comes from my grandfather, who escaped from the Netherlands during the Second World War and got to London by going to sea with the merchant navy. He has the most fascinating stories.

Life in Full Colour

Creative Channels

Right and opposite
At every turn, bold colour is used
to enliven the boat, from the
swathes of fabric that hang above
the bed to the fishermen's
lamps beside it, which are cosiest,
Jeanne says, with little lights
in them.

Life in Full Colour

Left
The wheelhouse leads down to the main living area below.

Opposite
Schuit looks at home against Rotterdam's modern canalside buildings.

Grand Design
Schuit, Netherlands

In these early years of the 21st century, achieving a healthy work/life balance is the ultimate goal, but that is exactly what Babs and Emile Estourgie have achieved on *Schuit*, an elegant Belgian Spits barge moored in Rotterdam. Swapping a tiny 60 m² (646 sq ft) house for a 200 m² (2,153 sq ft) boat has given them a spacious, light-filled home, as well as room to work and study. Yet that wasn't quite the original intention.

Grand Design

'We really just wanted to buy a boat for holidays, something like a little cabin cruiser,' Babs explains. 'But it grew bigger.'

Ship's companion

Life on board is a great adventure for a curious cat, but we have learned to make certain parts of the ship inaccessible. Kees went missing, and after an hour of searching, we found him under the wooden floor near the trusses. He was covered in grease, and found the shower that followed very unpleasant.

In addition to the dogs on shore, there are also lots of aquatic animals to see from the safety of the ship: a fish jumping up, a swan passing close by. And yes, Kees also has his own life jacket if we go sailing.

Emile smiles. 'It exploded. But that was partly for practical reasons: we didn't have enough money for a house and could only afford a small flat, which wasn't what we wanted. When we started looking at boats, we quickly realized that we had options. We also wanted a project that would unite us. Babs's work had been taking her one way and mine in another, and *Schuit* was something we could work on together. And with both of us being designers, it seemed natural.'

Indeed. The Estourgies are married not only to each other, but also to the world of design. Emile is a sought-after goldsmith, architectural model-maker and furniture restorer, while Babs, originally a graphic designer and stylist, is now a lecturer at the prestigious Graphic Lyceum Rotterdam. Both belong to the knowledge circle of Dutch designers and architects that includes Vincent De Rijk, Rem Koolhaas and Irma Boom.

Let loose on their new barge, the couple made use of their creative flair to come up with a glorious fusion of loft-style living and mid-century design, with high ceilings and open spaces, and joyful splashes of bold colour breaking up the otherwise calm aesthetic. Emile has an airy workshop, while Babs has ample quiet space to study for her teaching degree at the art academy. The outside deck even boasts a small pool, which is mainly used by the couple as a sheltered seating area.

Creative Channels

Schuit gives Babs and Emile space to live, work and play, room to flourish, both separately and together – Maslow's hierarchy of needs floating serenely in an inner-city dock.

'When we bought her, the guts were all in place, including the Crittall windows and the swimming pool,' Emile recalls. 'The previous owner had used the main area as his company office, so the living space was very cramped. But he did a perfect job with the essentials, from the electrics to the insulation, leaving us free to focus on opening up the interior.'

It had taken nearly four years to find *Schuit*, and even then, Emile was still feeling apprehensive about leaving a life on land. But he had promised Babs that if she could find a legal municipal mooring, he would make the leap. Unbeknownst to him, she had gone out and secured one through a contact. 'It was a charm offensive,' he says. 'She delighted them with funny stories and invited them on board for a swim, and they agreed to rent us the mooring for indefinite period of time.'

The couple are now firmly in their element on board *Schuit*, although Emile concedes that it hasn't always been plain sailing.

'There can be a bit of stress,' he admits. 'There's always something to do and a limited time in which to do it, both because of the work involved and the nature of living on a boat. At first it was quite a shock when we would clean a rivet and water would spurt in – it felt like we were sinking!'

Keeping traditions alive

In my on-board workshop is a table that is big enough to give lessons around. It is good to be able to pass on experience. Nobody knows how to do the basics anymore: how to file, how to saw. Restoration is a big part of my job, as people no longer have the patience to do it themselves. I've been working in this field for twenty years. It's a small world and quite a niche market. Being proficient in resins, metals and woods means you will always be sought after.

Every piece is equally important – it doesn't matter if it's for an architect, a museum or my neighbour. I just want to make nice things. It's all about emotion and real materials; Babs does that in her profession, too, as well as trading in mid-century design. We support each other pretty well in many ways.'

Do they ever think about moving back onto terra firma? 'Of course, we do,' Babs admits. 'But the problem is that Rotterdam is getting very crowded, and we would miss nature and the quiet. The building opposite has more people living in it than where Emile grew up. Perhaps we'll take *Schuit* with us and live in her in a field.'

Emile laughs. 'It's going to have to be a pretty special house to get us off this ship, which is why we'll probably die on her. We've got the freedom of living on the water with the ducks going by, yet we're still in the heart of the city. And if we do want to move, we can – we'll just take our floating home along with us. How great is that?'

Well, not quite. 'There is a small harbour where we can turn the boat, but it's crazy work,' he adds. 'On our last trip, we had to sail *Schuit* backwards to get her out of here. In the past, she would have been dragged round with a rope, but we're very careful with her. The guys who work in the harbour see her as the cargo ship she started life as, so they think we're wimps. But she's not an easy boat to get out of the harbour – we need to hire a good captain with good insurance! We don't want to bump her or damage her in any way. She's our home.'

Left
Neat, understated touches include vintage Hans Boodt hat mannequins, reminiscent of sculptures by Brancusi.

Opposite
The serene bedroom, white and minimally furnished, is the ideal place for the couple to unwind after days at work filled with stimulation, colour and images.

Creative Channels

Grand Design

194   Creative Channels

Above
The kitchen features floating
worktops and mobile furniture;
a 1970s white side table by
Marcello Siard provides extra
storage.

Right
Throughout the interior, Babs's
love of design punctuates
every room, from the barstools
designed by Lucci and Paolo
Orlandini to the 'Nesso' table
lamp from Artemide.

Opposite
The inside space has been
organized to ensure there is
'room to flourish, separately
and together'. The sheet and
wire roller is in daily use,
and reinforces the industrial
aesthetic.

Grand Design

Left
High ceilings make the interior feel spacious and allow natural light to flood in. The windows look onto the sunken terrace, which in summer can be used as a swimming pool.

Below
The dining area doubles as Babs's workroom, with a 1960s table by Cees Braakman for Pastoe and chairs are by Schroder & Henzelmann.

Opposite
A 'Moonboat' chair is suspended in front of a model of a passenger ship from the 1950s, a family heirloom from Babs's father. 'When there is a storm and the ship moves, you bounce along with the waves,' Babs says.

Creative Channels

Grand Design

Creative Channels

Right and opposite
Emile's well-equipped workshop
allows full scope for his work as
a goldsmith. The semi-industrial
doors ensure it is out of sight
once the working day is over.

Below left
Emile's prototypes and models,
made from materials such
as polyester and brass, sit side
by side with experimental
coloured resins.

Below right
Splashes of colour brighten up
the entrance to the lower deck.

Grand Design

Creative Channels

Living History
LV93, UK

Few seagoing vessels are built for such a single, vital purpose as a lightship. Since 1731, when the first one was anchored off the Nore in the Thames Estuary, these tough little workhorses have been stationed close to some of the world's most hazardous waters. Had a lightship not been on constant watch, those shoals and sandbanks would have lured thousands of ships and their crews to destruction.

Left
The couple's daughter showed an immediate fascination with the vessel and its infinite potential as a playground.

Opposite
The stout, proud lines of *LV93*: the search for a lightship became, in its owner's words, 'something of an obsession'.

Above
The boat's rugged aesthetic has been preserved; the deck makes a wonderfully open play area.

Left
Nautical details; the owners worked closely with some of London's last watermen and local metalworkers and carpenters before gentrification displaced them.

Opposite
Michele spent years restoring *LV93*, before sympathetically converting it into a home and photography studio.

Creative Channels

Living History

Creative Channels

Time and technology have changed the maritime landscape since the glory days of the lightships, with smarter radar steering vessels clear of otherwise fatal traps, and those still in existence are mostly fully automated floating robots. But the day of the lightship has not yet passed: a new generation of romantics has recognized the history and allure of this most industrial of crafts, and turned some of them into unusual and exciting homes.

Photographer Michele Turriani was an early convert, although he might not have known the boat that initially set him off on his quest was the direct descendant of that very first lightship.

'I fell in love with them soon after my arrival in London in 1992,' Michele says. 'I tend to discover and connect with cities by exploring them on foot, and one day I came across *LV89*, *The Nore*, when she was moored at St Katharine Docks, downstream of the Tower of London. I had never seen a historic lightship before, and was captivated by its formidable charm and character. I found three for sale at a breaker's yard in Portsmouth, but at the time the logistical challenges were too much. I shelved the project for ten years – although I had the plans of one of them, *LV12*, hanging in my living room for all of that time.'

Memories and reconnections

My lightship is many things to me: a home, a workplace, a restoration project. I do lots of photoshoots on board – for *Vogue*, *World of Interiors*, and others – and Cate Blanchett, the Arctic Monkeys, Mumford & Sons and Bond girl Olga Kurylenko have all been on board at one time or another. I like to think that we have brought fashion, celebrity and art to the Royal Docks. While I'm photographing them, people reminisce about relatives who worked in and around the docks. That's one of the lovely things about the ship: it triggers recollections and memories. Being based on the water somehow draws people in; they come to share their stories. It's a series of reconnections that encompasses the place, time and people.

Left
The boat's open, industrial spaces are an ideal backdrop for numerous photo and film shoots. Its original features have been retained and restored.

Opposite
Michele at work in the studio; he is known for his celebrity portraiture and large, floral still-life compositions.

Living History

After a friend bought a Dutch barge in 2002, Michele's passion was reignited. 'I started looking for lightships again, and found *LV23* for sale in Liverpool,' he remembers. 'I did a huge amount of research and planning, and eventually secured a London mooring, only to lose out to another buyer. But less than two weeks later, I was told that *LV93* and *LV95* were coming up for auction. By then my interest had reached full-blown obsession. When I first saw *LV93*, it was a magical experience. She had just come out of service, and – unlike the other lightships I'd seen – had been automated and modified to operate with solar power. Much of the early machinery and interiors had been removed, but the mahogany furniture was still in the cabins. The rest of the space was a blank canvas, and suited my needs for a live/work space perfectly.'

On board, there is no noise at all – apart from the planes. It's a remarkable oasis of silence and weirdness, with all sorts of wildlife. You can open the door to hear a screeching sound, and look up to see peregrine falcons flirting on the corner of the derelict Millennium Mills building. They have even fledged two young up on the roof. The Thames was declared almost biologically dead in the 1950s, but it has since recovered and harbour seals have been spotted on the southern edge of the Royal Docks. Eel numbers have also increased, and they bring in a lot of hungry birds to the river bank. We know that all this isolation is temporary, so for now we are cherishing this in-between state.

The conversion was a long process, especially as renovating a ship presents challenges never normally encountered in conventional buildings. The wheelhouse, for example, had been removed in the late 1980s, and was rebuilt to the original proportions, and the windows, lamps and electrical fittings are marine or industrial salvage. Michele worked with local craftsmen to source materials from warehouses near his mooring at Trinity Buoy Wharf in East London, much of which was rescued just before the buildings were redeveloped.

Most of the work was completed in time for Michele and his wife Storme to celebrate their wedding on board. Her influence provided some finishing touches. 'There is a stripped-metal theme running throughout,' Michele adds, 'but Storme introduced textures and fabrics that soften and complement the industrial feel.'

The couple and their daughter Océane now divide their time between their house on the Kent coast and *LV93*, their London home and workplace.

Living History

Below
A study in metals: a 19th-century
French bath is complemented
by surface-mounted copper
plumbing and industrial valves.

Opposite
Career opportunities: daughter
Océane practises her parents'
profession on her father.

'I had always intended the ship to be a location for photoshoots, as well as a studio,' Michele says. 'The metal shutters in the master bathroom open onto the sitting room, so I can set up lighting and cameras from more angles, and hatches in the floor can be opened up to shoot down into the studio below. As photographers, we're aware of even the subtlest changes in light quality. Boats are continuously moving, and new light effects are always emerging. I have spent an inordinate amount of time looking out of the window of a ship at the changing weather and its effect on the water.'

But it's the boat herself that provides Michele with some of his favourite visual feasts. 'There is a point in the sitting room from which you can see the full length of *LV93*,' he says, 'from the top of the bow to the flag mast on the stern. These nerdy little things give me the greatest pleasure.'

Creative Channels

Living History

Make Do &
Mend in the East End
De Walvisch, UK

If all boats say something about their owners –
which they surely do – it will come as no
surprise that the owners of *De Walvisch* are
larger than life, eccentric and individual,
just like the vessel that has been their home for
the past ten years. Rebuilt and restored
by the artists known as Zatorski & Zatorski
(Thomas and Angel to their friends), this
Dutch sailing clipper, which once carried eels
from Holland and is now moored in East
London, brims with the odd and the unexpected.

Creative Channels

This page
The boat is berthed at Hermitage
Moorings, a co-operative
entirely self-funded by members.
The close-knit community is
committed to the preservation
of historic craft.

Opposite
The Zatorskis on board:
'The most important thing about
owning a boat is knowing
when to get off' says Thomas.

Make Do & Mend in the East End

Left
The galley and dining area is a compact but functional space, with walls covered in brass and blackboard paint.

Below left
Intelligently curated touches are everywhere on *De Walvisch*, from a top hat to a military jacket.

Below right
Everything had to be made to fit – as seen in the bedrooms, where storage and space to study were squeezed in.

Opposite
A shaft of sunlight streams through the passageway, highlighting the couple's collection of books and brass panels on the ceiling.

Make Do & Mend in the East End

Right
Angel on board; the boat has taken the couple on a 'journey with no particular end in view'.

Below
From shoes to period maps, the boat's interior is a rich and textual treat.

Below right
The couple's tastes are eccentric, but always engaging. 'We make work about things that interest us, and live with objects we like,' Angel says.

Creative Channels

The idea of water-borne living had been percolating for a while before the couple, who met while both were exhibiting at an Israeli art show, took the plunge. They had a studio in Islington overlooking a canal, and the seed was planted. 'In 2000 we sold a piece of work and bought a pretty crap narrowboat,' Thomas admits. 'A crumbly first home on the water.'

The attraction of living 'slightly under the radar' was firmly embedded. Thomas and Angel are both obsessed with history – both of London and of their boat – and when the opportunity to buy *De Walvisch* arose, they jumped at it. The location they eventually washed up in – the 'village' of Wapping, a small enclave in the Docklands area of the city – also mattered. Many of the older, established families go back generations, with decades spent working in and around the river.

'History is around every corner in this part of town,' Angel says. 'Wapping is still something of a proper East End community.'

Art and culture on the water

We were interested in the role of ships as a representation of discovery and adventure, and a go-between from this world to the next, so we decided to create a 'living artwork' vessel. This led to the *De Walvisch* project, and later to *The Cultureship*, a non-profit curatorial venture that allows us to commission and produce high-impact artworks with a maritime context. One such collaboration was *1513: A Ships' Opera*, a water-borne performance created with the sculptor Richard Wilson. It was the centrepiece of the 2013 Thames Festival, which culminated in a musical score written for an armada of historic vessels, and played out with steamwhistles, bells, horns, hooters, sirens and cannon.

The purchase and restoration of the boat was, the couple note, a journey 'with no particular end in view'. The interior is made up of largely reclaimed materials, and everything was made to fit. They see this ability to improvise – to make do and mend – as being firmly in the traditional skipper's role, who had to solve

Make Do & Mend in the East End

Creative Channels

any problem that arose at sea, in dock or on the river. The initial rebuild was overseen while the couple were based in the Netherlands, where they learned to sail and navigate, and work continues at a lesser rate in London. 'It never really ends,' Thomas notes, ruefully. 'Everything gets washed up and taken away, and every day is new.'

It is the details that really beguile visitors. In the bow-windowed bedroom is the former captain's cabin, with a bespoke solid teak double bed. A solid brass porthole from SS *Transylvania* allows a view to the chain locker and bow of the ship, and the hatch to the master berth is from HMS *Intrepid*, a ship that was involved in the retaking of the Falklands. An antique submarine sink completes the find-and-fit aesthetic wonderfully.

Thomas and Angel were instrumental is building up the co-operative mooring – Hermitage Moorings, just east of Tower Bridge – they now share with seventeen other boats. The site was owned by a tug master – 'one of the last of the breed' – and a condition is that all boats have to be fully functional. No floating homes here, moveable only with the aid of another boat. 'It's something of a microcosm of society, a great mix of people,' Thomas says. The couple hold monthly salons, where guests – who do not know each other – are invited to talk, eat and drink, and reaffirm their devotion to the unexpected. The aim, he adds, is to create 'an evening where a banker talks about art, and an artist talks about money.'

Life on the water: it's for those who think differently, who like to write their own rules. Or, as this mischievous and energetic pair put it, 'boat life is always a subset of people.' Perhaps this is never more true than on board *De Walvisch*.

Steeped in local history

Because of its proximity to the water, Wapping has strong maritime links that can still be seen along the riverside today. The neighbourhood fascinates us, as it was geared around the river and was inhabited by sailors, boat-builders, victuallers and craftsmen of all kinds well into the 20th century, along with representatives of all the other trades that supported seafarers. These people belonged to the river: they knew it like the back of their hands, and could navigate it by its smell and the sounds of the bells, the same way a seagull will use the Thames as a highway to navigate across London. It is a fitting home for *De Walvisch*.

Right
The wash basin was salvaged from a submarine.

Opposite
The interior is a journey back in time: the bed is hand-crafted and made from solid teak.

Make Do & Mend in the East End

Creative Channels

Make Do & Mend in the East End

Previous pages
The kitchen illustrates the couple's make-do-and-mend approach, with teak salvaged from school lab desks.

Below
The dining table is set for one of the couple's salon evenings, where guests gather together to feast on new ideas.

Right
A taxidermy saddle-billed stork is one of the many curiosities to be found on board.

Opposite
Moored just yards from Tower Bridge, *De Walvisch* stands proud against the London skyline.

Creative Channels

Make Do & Mend in the East End

Directory

Altar (pp. 32–41)
Rodrigo Martins
São Paolo, Brazil
@altar.br
oaltar.com.br

Boat With No Name
(pp. 52–63)
Philip Newton
Seattle, Washington, USA
philipnewtonphoto.com

Bosco (pp. 164–75)
Claire Bunten and
Alistair Langhorne
London, UK
@labarchitects
labarchitects.com/
practice

De Walvisch (pp. 210–21)
Thomas and
Angel Zatorski
Wapping, London, UK
zatorskiandzatorski.com

Feniks (pp. 12–21)
Pieter Kool and
Stefanie Hakkesteegt
Amsterdam, Netherlands
carbon-studio.eu
schoonschipamsterdam.org

Graaf Floris V (pp. 142–53)
Annelies Dorsman
Amsterdam, Netherlands
@dirksdotter
dirksdotter.com

Lady Cat (pp. 110–17)
Jo Pardue
Kent, UK
@jopardue12

Le Cid (pp. 64–73)
Agnès Combes Bernageau
Paris, France
@bobo_on_a_boat

Lisbeth (pp. 74–79)
Sarah Mittler and
Marco Eckert
Wiesbaden, Germany
@hausbootlisbeth
hausboot-lisbeth.de

LV93 (pp. 200–9)
Michele Turriani and
Storme Sabine
London, UK
@michele_turriani
@lightship93
@stormesabine

Mini (pp. 42–49)
Anibal Guiser Gleyzer
Buenos Aires, Argentina
@econautico

Oldenburg (pp. 130–41)
Lis and Ove Nilsson
Denmark
@christina.kayser.o

Raumschiff (pp. 118–27)
Thea Sparmeier and
Moritz Wussow
Potsdam, Germany
@raum.schiff
raumschiff.studio

Reetainer (pp. 22–31)
Max McMurdo
Bedfordshire, UK
@maxreestore
maxmcmurdo.co.uk

Schuit (pp. 188–99)
Babs and Emile Estourgie
Rotterdam, Netherlands
@schipschuit

Soggybottom Shanty
(pp. 104–9)
Siva Aiken
South Carolina, USA
@sivaaiken

Stødig (pp. 94–103)
Guylee Simmonds and
David Schnabel
@arcticlifeboat
arctic-lifeboat.com

This One Floats (pp. 154–63)
Christina Miles and
Rohan Tully
London, UK
@thisonefloats
islayachts.com

Zazi Houseboat (pp. 178–87)
Jeanne de Kroon
Amsterdam, Netherlands
@jeannedekroon
jeannedekroon.com

Photo credits

6t Christina Kayser O (Styling: Rikke Graff Juel); 6b Tom Peppiatt; 7 Christina Kayser O (Styling: Rikke Graff Juel); 8–9 David Schnabel and Guylee Simmonds; 12–21 Muk Van Lil; 22–31 Brent Darby; 32–41 Mel Audi; 42–9 Daniel Fernández Harper; 52–63 Rafael Soldi; 64–73 Tom Peppiatt; 74–9 Stefan Marquardt; 80–91 Mike Pickles; 94–103 David Schnabel and Guylee Simmonds; 104–9 Shivaun deLisser; 110–17 Jo Pardue; 118–27 Manuela Clemens; 130–41 Christina Kayser O (Styling: Rikke Graff Juel); 142, 143 Muk Van Lil; 144–5 Tom Peppiatt; 147–53 Muk Van Lil; 154–63 Tom Peppiatt; 164–75 Chris Everard, Lab Architects; 178–80t Muk Van Lil; 180b Tom Peppiatt; 181–7 Muk Van Lil; 188–99 Tom Peppiatt; 200–9 © Michele Turriani and Storme Sabine; 210–21 Roger Bool

About the author

Portland Mitchell's career as a stylist spans over twenty years. She has been coordinating editor for *Country Homes & Interiors* and style editor for *Living, Etc* magazines. Since going freelance, she has worked as on-set stylist for clients such as Harrods, John Lewis, Laura Ashley, Arlo & Jacob and the White Company in the UK, Amazon in South Africa and Q Home Decor in Dubai. Along with editorial projects for *Homes & Gardens*, *Coast* and *Easy Living* magazines, she has worked on homes brochures for Homebase, Tesco and B&Q. In 2001 she won the Crown Stylist of the Year Award.

Acknowledgments

This book was possible not just because Thames & Hudson took a punt on me, a total novice in the book world, but also because of the support of the many brilliantly creative people who helped me navigate my way through this vast learning curve: Dominic Bradbury; my friends and translators Vicente Ben, Carla Mendes and Vera Cunha; the enthusiastic photographers who captured both the homes and the personalities of their owners; the sympathetic writing skills of David Lancaster, Patrick Stoddart and Gill Mullins, as well as my agent Sarah Kaye, whose knowledge has been my constant rock.

Finally, and most importantly, I give thanks to everyone whose houseboat, shantyboat, cargo ship, lightship or lifeboat we feature in these pages. They are visioned enough to know that many of us are searching for solace with style (the very best of both worlds) and have opened their cabin doors to allow us a tantalizing glimpse of life on the waves.

To my family: Stuart, Olive, Philippa,
David and Bonnie

First published in the United Kingdom
in 2023 by Thames & Hudson Ltd,
181A High Holborn, London WC1V 7QX

First published in the United States of America
in 2023 by Thames & Hudson Inc.,
500 Fifth Avenue, New York, New York 10110

Designed by Studio Wan

British Library Cataloguing-in-Publication Data
A catalogue record for this book is available from
the British Library

Library of Congress Control Number 2022945741

ISBN 978-0-500-02421-8

Printed and bound in China by Toppan Leefung
Printing Limited

Be the first to know about our new releases,
exclusive content and author events by visiting
thamesandhudson.com
thamesandhudsonusa.com
thamesandhudson.com.au

On the cover: Front *This One Floats*, UK (main photo:
Christina Miles; inset: Eva Pruchova/Shutterstock);
Back *Altar*, Brazil (photo: Mel Audi)